CONTEMPORARY WRITERS

General Editors
MALCOLM BRADBURY
and
CHRISTOPHER BIGSBY

MALCOLM LOWRY

MALCOLM
LOWRY

RONALD BINNS

METHUEN
LONDON AND NEW YORK

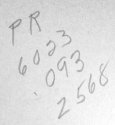

For my parents

First published in 1984 by
Methuen & Co. Ltd
11 New Fetter Lane, London EC4P 4EE
Published in the USA by
Methuen & Co.
in association with Methuen, Inc.
733 Third Avenue, New York, NY 10017

© 1984 Ronald Binns

Typeset by Rowland Phototypesetting Ltd
Printed in Great Britain by
Richard Clay (The Chaucer Press) Ltd
Bungay, Suffolk

British Library Cataloguing in Publication Data

Binns, Ronald
Malcolm Lowry. – (Contemporary writers)
1. Lowry Malcolm – Criticism and interpretation
I. Title   II. Series
823'.912   PR6023.O96Z/

ISBN 0-416-37750-5

Library of Congress Cataloging in Publication Data

Binns, Ronald, 1948–
Malcolm Lowry.
(Contemporary writers)
Bibliography: p.
1. Lowry, Malcolm, 1909-1957 – Criticism and interpretation.
I. Title.   II. Series.   PR6023.O96Z568   1984
813'.54   84-1080
ISBN 0-416-37750-5 (pbk.)

CONTENTS

GENERAL EDITORS' PREFACE

The contemporary is a country which we all inhabit, but there is little agreement as to its boundaries or its shape. The serious writer is one of its most sensitive interpreters, but criticism is notoriously cautious in offering a response or making a judgement. Accordingly, this continuing series is an endeavour to look at some of the most important writers of our time, and the questions raised by their work. It is, in effect, an attempt to map the contemporary, to describe its aesthetic and moral topography.

The series came into existence out of two convictions. One was that, despite all the modern pressures on the writer and on literary culture, we live in a major creative time, as vigorous and alive in its distinctive way as any that went before. The other was that, though criticism itself tends to grow more theoretical and apparently indifferent to contemporary creation, there are grounds for a lively aesthetic debate. This series, which includes books written from various standpoints, is meant to provide a forum for that debate. By design, some of those who have contributed are themselves writers, willing to respond to their contemporaries; others are critics who have brought to the discussion of current writing the spirit of contemporary criticism or simply a conviction, forcibly and coherently argued, for the contemporary significance of their subjects. Our aim, as the series develops, is to continue to explore the works of major post-war writers – in fiction, drama and poetry – over an international range, and thereby to illuminate not only those works but also in some degree the artistic, social and moral assumptions on which they rest. Our wish is that, in their very variety of approach and emphasis, these books will stimulate interest in and understanding of the vitality of a living literature which, because it is contemporary, is especially ours.

Norwich, England

MALCOLM BRADBURY
CHRISTOPHER BIGSBY

PREFACE AND
ACKNOWLEDGEMENTS

The retrieval of Malcolm Lowry's reputation has been a slow process. *Under the Volcano* (1947) had its admirers from the moment of publication, but for many years critical interest stayed tepid, particularly in Britain. There is some resemblance to the cases of Borges and Nabokov. It is easy to forget, of these two authors who today seem amongst our very greatest late moderns, that Borges published *Ficciones* as long ago as 1944, and that Nabokov was a largely unknown novelist until his sixtieth year.

If Lowry now seems less marginal than before, it is because some of the old certainties have gone. Ours is a pluralist culture and contemporary writing cannot be convicted of quietism in either technique or subject matter. The mix of metaphysics, opulent experimental prose and restless metafictional speculation which characterizes Lowry's best work no longer seems as freakish and fearful as (in some eyes) it used to. We can see, now, that *Under the Volcano* is one of those substantial, ambitious, achieved hybrid works like *Moby-Dick* or *Ulysses* which wrench apart the orthodoxies on which more timid fictions rest.

In his survey *Ninety-Nine Novels* (1984), Anthony Burgess asserts that 'By the end of the century *Under the Volcano* may be seen as one of its few authentic masterpieces'. Lowry's reputation has always been high with other novelists. The current Spanish paperback edition of *Under the Volcano* carries the recommendation from the South American writer Gabriel Garcia Márquez (winner of the 1982 Nobel Prize for

8

Literature) that it is 'probably the novel that I have read the most times in my life. I would like not to have to read it any more but that would be impossible, for I shall not rest until I have discovered where its hidden magic lies'. Novelists as diverse as William Styron, Brian Moore, Malcolm Bradbury, W. H. Gass and J. G. Farrell were, like Anthony Burgess, early admirers of Lowry's work; his contemporary significance cannot be in doubt.

Malcolm Lowry is a writer essentially remembered for one great book. Unlike other novelists of similar reputation (Sterne, Cervantes, Gogol, Goncharov, perhaps Melville) Lowry made his masterpiece elusive and unstable for us by returning to it and reworking it in the structure of his *œuvre*. Before 1960 Lowry was known, at best, only as the author of two published novels. The decade that followed saw a sequence of posthumous publications which included an important volume of stories, *Hear Us O Lord From Heaven Thy Dwelling Place* (1961), a novella, *Lunar Caustic* (1968), and two more novels, *Dark as the Grave Wherein My Friend is Laid* (1968) and *October Ferry to Gabriola* (1970). Some of these works are radically experimental in tenor, and give us a clearer picture of Lowry's Herculean struggle to rewrite and supersede his masterwork. There are signs that a younger generation of writers and critics are discovering in the post-*Volcano* fiction not autobiographical indulgence but *jouissance*, experimental rigour, an exemplary inventiveness.

In this book I have concentrated on what I regard as Lowry's best work, namely *Lunar Caustic, Under the Volcano, Dark as the Grave Wherein My Friend is Laid* and some of the late stories. I have said relatively little about Lowry's life, preferring to examine the ways in which Lowry related his fictional personae to society and history and gave them public meaning and significance. Malcolm Lowry believed that writing should not stand still but perpetually evolve, and with that in mind I have endeavoured to avoid repeating the following previously published material, where my earlier responses to Lowry's fiction and developing critical reputation may be found: 'Lowry', *The Ubyssey* (Vancouver), 27 September 1974, pp. 4 –5; 'Wrestling with Lowry', *Vancouver Sun*, 18 October 1974;

'Lowry's Anatomy of Melancholy', *Canadian Literature*, 64 (Spring 1975), pp. 8–23; 'The Lowry Fringe', *Canadian Literature*, 72 (Spring 1977), pp. 91–2; 'Beckett, Lowry and the Anti-Novel', in Malcolm Bradbury and David Palmer (eds), *The Contemporary English Novel* (London: Edward Arnold, 1979); 'Lowry Today', *Canadian Literature*, 84 (Spring 1980), pp. 108–10; 'Materialism and Magic in *Under the Volcano*', *Critical Quarterly*, 23, 1 (Spring 1981), pp. 21–32; 'Malcolm Lowry' in *Dictionary of Literary Biography*, *Vol. 15: British Novelists, 1930–1959, Part 1* (Detroit, Mich.: Gale, 1983).

I would like to express my gratitude to Roger Bromley, who first introduced me to *Under the Volcano*. Numerous other individuals have also helped to shape my understanding of Lowry's work. In Britain I'd particularly like to thank Vic Sage, Malcolm Bradbury, Brian O'Kill and Duncan Hadfield and, in Canada, Marketa Goetz-Stankiewicz, W. H. New and Gary Geddes. I am also indebted to Anne Yandle of the Special Collections Division of the Main Library at the University of British Columbia, and to Margerie Bonner Lowry for permission to quote from unpublished material. An award from the Commonwealth Scholarship and Fellowship Commission of London and Ottawa made it possible for me to travel to Vancouver and examine the Lowry manuscript collection of UBC.

The author and publisher would like to thank Penguin Books, Jonathan Cape and the executors of the Malcolm Lowry Estate for permission to quote from *Under the Volcano*, and Joseph Killorin and Yale University Press for permission to quote from *Selected Letters of Conrad Aiken* (1978).

London, England, 1984   RONALD BINNS

A NOTE ON THE TEXTS

Page references for quotations from Malcolm Lowry's writings are taken from the editions listed below. In the case of *Under the Volcano* two references have been given (except where pagination is identical); the first refers to the American edition, the second to the English paperback edition. The following abbreviations have been used:

U   *Ultramarine* (Revised edition. London: Jonathan Cape, 1963)

PAS   *Malcolm Lowry: Psalms and Songs*, ed. Margerie Lowry (New York: New American Library, 1975)

UTV   *Under the Volcano* (New York: Reynal & Hitchcock, 1947. Harmondsworth: Penguin, 1962)

HUOL   *Hear Us O Lord from Heaven Thy Dwelling Place* (London: Jonathan Cape, 1962)

DAG   *Dark as the Grave Wherein My Friend is Laid* (London: Jonathan Cape, 1969)

OF   *October Ferry to Gabriola* (London: Jonathan Cape, 1971)

SL   *The Selected Letters of Malcolm Lowry*, ed. Harvey Breit and Margerie Lowry (London: Jonathan Cape, 1967)

SP   *Selected Poems of Malcolm Lowry*, ed. Earle Birney (San Francisco: City Lights, 1962)

1

THE LOWRY MYTH

Talent and character may be innate; but the manner in which they develop, or fail to develop, depends on the writer's interaction with his environment, on his relationships with other human beings. (Georg Lukács, *The Meaning of Contemporary Realism*)

Malcolm Lowry occupies a strange position in modern writing. His career unfolded on the cultural and social margins, away from metropolitan centres of fashion and influence. Lowry's difficulties with publishers have become legendary. He completed and published only two novels in his lifetime (1909–57); in Britain both books were remaindered. Lowry's isolation as a writer was reinforced by his decision to lead, quite literally, a marginal existence. He was an expatriate, living much of his career outside urban society, amid the self-imposed hardships of a Canadian squatter settlement.

Out of all this has grown up the romantic image of Malcolm Lowry as an exemplary drop-out, the self-destructive dipsomaniac genius who sobered-up long enough to write *Under the Volcano* and who then faded into obscurity, a burned-out case. It is a misleading picture, but one which the novelist himself bears some responsibility for. Lowry was often mischievously keen to promote himself as a suffering and neglected genius. He explained that in his childhood he endured extraordinary cruelty (a claim indignantly refuted by his sole surviving brother, Russell). In fact he seems to have had a happy, conventional childhood. He was born in 1909, in New Brighton, Cheshire, the youngest of four brothers. Lowry's father was a Liverpool cotton-broker, 'a capitalist on the grand scale' (*SL*, p. 260). In 1911 the family moved to Caldy, on the other side of the Wirral peninsula, overlooking the sea and the Clwydian mountain range. The Lowrys were Methodists and the atmosphere at home was slightly sombre (opportunities nevertheless arose to develop enthusiasms like jazz records and silent films). Lowry *père* encouraged his boys to be sportsmen, and Malcolm became a competent golfer and tennis player. At the age of eight he followed in the footsteps of his brothers and was packed off, first to preparatory school, then to a minor public school. The psychic landscapes of Lowry's childhood reappear ambiguously in his fiction, partly viewed as an insufferable bourgeois nightmare, partly as a haunting lost Eden of innocence and happiness. (In later years Lowry converted his Wirral origins to Manx, emphasizing the symbolic nature of his links with the Isle of Man.)

This pattern of an orthodox upper-middle-class upbringing was first broken in 1927 when Lowry, determined to get 'experience' (his grandfather had been a ship's captain), sailed on 17 May as a deck-hand on the SS *Pyrrhus* to Yokohama. It was a voyage which was to become almost as crucial to Lowry's development as a writer as Melville's service on the whaler *Acushnet*. Lowry returned in October, chastened and disturbed by his encounter with hard physical labour, sex, class hostility and boredom. As a teenager Lowry had begun writing short comic stories for his school magazine (he had also rebelliously begun to engage in bouts of heavy drinking); now he had something more substantial to write about and promptly set to work on his first novel, *Ultramarine* (1933).

In the years that followed other crucial episodes and influences cast their shadows over his developing sensibility. In 1928 Lowry spent three months at a college in Bonn, where he developed a taste for German expressionism (see *SL*, pp. 238–9). The following year he travelled to New England to spend the summer with the American writer Conrad Aiken, who had agreed to tutor his young admirer in return for a fee. That autumn Lowry went up to St Catherine's College, Cambridge, and was almost immediately involved in scandal when a close friend, Paul Fitte, committed suicide in mysterious circumstances on 14 November. (Charlotte Haldane, the wife of a Cambridge don, later published a *roman à clef* about the tragedy, entitled *I Bring Not Peace* (1932).) At Cambridge Lowry encountered figures like I. A. Richards and William Empson, who were helping to lay the foundations of modern critical approaches to literature and comparative literature. He also found an English faculty enthusiastically committed to contemporary writing. *Ultramarine* registers the impact of Lowry's Cambridge years and sometimes reads as if the author has ransacked his set books over a three-year period.

After Cambridge Lowry set out on a series of romantic journeys which took him yet further from his bourgeois origins. His voyage to New York in 1934 seems in part to have stemmed from his love of jazz and Melville. Lowry's taste for the 'white jazz' of Bix Beiderbecke, Frankie Trumbauer, Eddie Lang and Joe Venuti was formed in the 1920s and took him to the bars of Harlem. But New York was also the city where Melville had struggled to complete *Moby-Dick* (1851) and had later spent almost twenty years in virtual obscurity. Lowry's own adolescent sea-voyage and his Liverpudlian connections had given him a special affinity with Melville's *Redburn* (1849), the 'sailor-boy confessions and reminiscences of the Son-of-a-Gentleman' making his first voyage. But he was also drawn to Melville 'because of his failure as a writer and his whole outlook generally. His failure for some reason absolutely fascinated me' (*SL*, p. 197).

Later Lowry moved on to Hollywood, Mexico and, finally, Canada. These experiences provided the substance of his novels and stories, which are almost always based upon journeys. But in Lowry's fiction journeys are never simple. Although always located in a naturalistic twentieth-century world they turn into journeys of the soul, guilt-ridden pilgrimages through a landscape of nightmare in pursuit of a remote and elusive redemption. He eventually planned to produce an epic sequence entitled 'The Voyage That Never Ends', incorporating most of his life's work and based around the theme of life as a spiritual quest.

In Lowry's fiction the metaphysical quest is always entangled with two other complicating elements. The first is his acute awareness of the fictionality of narrative. Lowry's stories restlessly signal their own artifice, aware both of their impure autobiographical origins and of the suffocating pressure of literary tradition. The shadow of four great prototypes of journey hangs over Lowry's writing: Dante's descent into hell in the *Inferno*, the satirical peregrinations of Cervantes's Don Quixote and Gogol's Mr Chichikov, and Ahab's visionary quest in *Moby-Dick*. Lowry was haunted by the notion of writing a masterpiece which would surpass or at least equal these classics, but he was also tormented by the idea that his work had a second-hand plagiaristic quality and that he had nothing new to contribute to literature. Lowry felt this strongly because of the second problematic dimension engaged with in his fiction: how to relate the quest (often based on rather narrow personal experience) to the world at large. In *Permanent Red* (1960), John Berger suggests that the constant problem for the modern artist is to find themes which connect him (or her) with his (or her) public. This was a particularly acute dilemma for Malcolm Lowry. There are in Lowry's career, as Malcolm Bradbury has observed, 'numerous uneasy signs of a creative direction never fully achieved, a bewilderment about the public meanings of his own type of creativity.'[1] Lowry's favourite fictional persona was that of the outcast and suffering romantic, but casting this into a meaningful form presented real difficulties. At the beginning of his career it was partly a matter of living out the myth and the fiction would follow. Later this came to seem too narrow and impoverished a resource.

Lowry relished the role of bohemian drifter and poverty-stricken genius. Not everyone who knew him well was impressed by this. In 1940 his friend the poet Conrad Aiken wrote caustically that he was looking forward to finding out 'what truth or lies constituted the now quite alarmingly hypertrophied Legend of the Lowry which has been built up. . . . Seen in its queer total, I can assure you, it doesn't make sense:

it's the goddamndest farrago of inconsistencies I ever did see, and hollow as a cream puff.'[2] In reality Lowry was the family remittance man, surviving on a generous allowance from his long-suffering businessman father. But Lowry's affiliation with the stereotype of the neglected outsider proved hard to shake off. When *Under the Volcano* was widely acclaimed in the United States, Lowry became masochistically obsessed with a single dissenting review which accused him of imitating Joyce, Hemingway, Thomas Wolfe and other styles in fashion. When the book became a commercial success Lowry proclaimed the situation intolerable, 'like some horrible disaster' (*SP*, p. 78).

On other occasions fate intervened to lend substance to the Lowry myth. The manuscript of his first novel *Ultramarine* was stolen and the book had to be rewritten. When it was finally published, sales were poor. Lowry spent the rest of the decade desperately trying to get something substantial published. He completed a collection of verse entitled 'The Lighthouse Invites the Storm', but it was never published (Aiken complained about the bad influence of 'the Complex Boys, these adolescent audens spenders (*sic*) with all their pretty little dexterities, their negative safety, their indoor marxmanship'[3]). Lowry submitted for publication a short novel, 'The Last Address' (about a young Englishman's obsession with Melville), but it was turned down. Robert Linscott of Houghton Mifflin found it 'tainted with genius' but unpublishable, wishing that Lowry had expended his talents 'on a more useful theme'.[4] Arriving in Mexico at the end of 1936 Lowry almost immediately began writing *Under the Volcano*; by 1940 he had expanded it from a short novel into a much longer narrative. At this point it was still a rather flat and feeble composition which only superficially resembled the novel we now know by that name. Lowry's *magnum opus* of the decade was actually *In Ballast to the White Sea*. Aiken read it in 1937 and described it as 'really remarkable. . . . Too much of it, and directionless, but for sheer tactile richness and beauty of prose texture a joy to swim in.'[5] This novel (fully described in Lowry's long letter to David Markson of 25 August 1951 (*SL*, pp. 247–66)) was submitted to Aiken's agent, who 'couldn't make head nor tail of it' and 'thought it not a commercial prospect.'[6] The manuscript, still

17

unpublished, was destroyed in a fire in 1944. Lowry's wry comment that his correspondence 'may sometimes sound like Mr Micawber's' (*SL*, p. 173) appears as something of an understatement. Much of Lowry's other work was never completed, and when he died of an overdose of sleeping tablets in 1957 the myth had come true. His two novels were out of print; he really was a forgotten and neglected writer. As Conrad Aiken put it: 'to have manufactured such a myth, and turned himself into it, was perhaps a feat of literary *trompe-l'œil* without parallel.'[7]

Colourful and compelling though it may be the Lowry myth is something of a distraction. Lowry's letters and fiction are equivocal as sources of biographical data, and to designate his writing as 'autobiographical' is unhelpful if it is taken to mean (as it usually is) writing that is self-indulgently and single-mindedly confessional, finding its form by accident.

'Strange Comfort Afforded by the Profession' (1953), almost the last thing Lowry published in his lifetime, addresses these questions of literary identity directly. A writer named Wilderness visits the house in Rome where Keats died. He then moves on to a bar, where he broodingly examines two of his notebooks. Wilderness reflectively sifts through a vast inventory of apparently disparate events and historical figures in order to anatomize his own artistic isolation. For Wilderness the romantic sensibility is central to his identity as a writer. The eternal truths are suffering, neglect, alienation, exile, poverty, despair and the indifference or incomprehension of society at large. The lives of numerous individuals associated in one way or another with Rome, and especially those of Keats, Edgar Allan Poe and Gogol, persuasively testify to this. But as Wilderness contemplates his notebooks he begins to interrogate the notion of the artist as doomed outsider. Were Poe's letters (he wonders) really intended simply as private communications? Even at a moment of great extremity 'Poe must have felt that he was transcribing the story that was E. A. Poe. [. . .] Some of Keats's own published letters were not different' (*HUOL*, p. 107).[8]

The *poète maudit* is shown to stand at a slightly unscrupulous angle to his apparent sufferings, scrutinizing them with

18

cold artistic detachment, an artificer who never quite lets on what he is up to. The posture, Wilderness decides, is not only a fiction; it is also absurd. Writers cannot stand apart from society. They, like everyone else (including the President of the United States), occasionally require the services of a dentist. Wilderness himself is not a free spirit but is dependent on patronage in the form of a Guggenheim Fellowship. He notes, too, that Keats's house stands near the less romantic but necessary American Express office. Wilderness despondently recognizes that the grand heroic life-style of Keats and Shelley is gone from the world. Modern writers dress like bank clerks and very often *are* bank clerks. How can one be a romantic hero in modern capitalist society, where the writer's sensitive eye is likely to be assaulted by headache adverts, Pepsi signs or the grotesque, deflating presence of the Bone Dry Fertilizer Company? The romantic sensibility is deconstructed, shattered into comic fragments, forcing Wilderness into 'a loud laugh' (*HUOL*, p. 113).

Pain still exists for a writer like Wilderness, but it is held at a distance and rendered into comedy. Though he suffers slightly from paranoia and is afraid of being mistaken for a spy (as the Consul is in *Under the Volcano*) no one bothers him. Though, like the Consul, he haunts the places of darkness and obscurity, he finds the darkness of Keats's house 'comforting' (*HUOL*, p. 100). The bar in the underground grotto altogether lacks the murderous threat of the Farolito. When we first encounter Wilderness he is poised on some steps 'above the flower stall' (*HUOL*, p. 99) – a homely location at the opposite extreme from that terrain which lies 'under the volcano'.

The story contains an unexpected twist at the end. Having exhibited the comic absurdity of the romantic sensibility, Lowry has Wilderness suddenly discover a passage of 'shaky and hysterical' (*HUOL*, p. 110) writing in his second notebook. It turns out to be the draft of a letter written several years earlier, in Seattle. The sufferings described in this letter triumphantly identify Wilderness as the modern heir of the romantic *poètes maudits*. The story ends with Wilderness, firmly established as a modern Keats, darkly enjoying a 'relatively pleasurable' (*HUOL*, p 113) fit of mock-tubercular coughing.

The identification is made and the possibilities of the romantic sensibility are reaffirmed for modern writing, but a difference remains. The contemporary *poète maudit* is, in Lowry's version, possessed of a peculiarly post-modern consciousness. Writing can no longer pretend to be transparent or innocent. Artifice and fictionality must be acknowledged in all their forms. That includes a comic exposure of apparently non-fictional forms like autobiography or letters.

Twenty years earlier, in his first novel *Ultramarine*, Lowry displayed his aesthetic anxieties in a rather more febrile fashion. Dana Hilliot is a young man working on a freighter en route to Japan. As the book's Chaucer epigraph indicates, Hilliot has deliberately spurned the claims of family life in order to embark on a lonely romantic quest for authenticity through suffering. It soon becomes apparent that the identity which Hilliot is really seeking is to be a writer, though this is something he is anxious to deny, almost hysterically:

> Read my collected works first, several thousand volumes, including the much-discussed *Othello*, all tightly bound, paying special attention to my masterpiece, *How To Be Happy Though Dead*. (*U*, p. 102)

Hilliot, initially rejected by the other sailors, overcomes the barrier of class and moves from alienation to integration. At the end he is promoted to fireman and admitted to the stokehold. This is a hellish below-decks world of 'flaming nightmares, firelit demons' (*U*, p. 171), ruled over by 'a fire-bright fiend' (*U*, p. 23), a Russian named Nikolai (Nikolai Gogol, perhaps). Paradoxically, in discovering communion with the crew, his identity as a *poète maudit* is symbolically established. Earlier, Hilliot had recalled his pathetic inability as a schoolboy to create a regular hexagon. By the end he is able to step forward as an authentic romantic hero and write the six-chaptered *Ultramarine*, that 'self-conscious first novel' (*U*, p. 96) which previously he had scorned.

As a portrait of the artist as a young man *Ultramarine* has its limitations. Hilliot's experiences on the long voyage often seem too slight and inconsequential to bear the significance which the narrative seeks to attach to them. The characterization is weak and the narrative momentum sluggish. A reviewer in *The Times Literary Supplement* (13 July 1933) found the novel and its hero exasperating, '– the exasperation being the more acute that the youngster was of the rare type that does some of its thinking in Greek'.

To contemporary eyes what power the novel still possesses probably lies precisely in those highly charged passages of interior monologue which the reviewer was complaining about. Here Lowry gives free rein to his imagination, letting loose an often brilliant sequence of parodies, fantasies and intoxicating word-games. The novel is a remarkable *tour de force* for a writer of only twenty-three. But *Ultramarine* also shows that though attracted to dream, reverie, fantasy, hallucination, Lowry had not found an appropriate form in which to express himself. The novel's exuberant, anarchic undergraduate humour sits awkwardly next to the naturalistic dialogue of the sailors; in the end the thrust towards fantasy and comic invention is retarded by an inadequate realist framework.

*

At the heart of *Ultramarine* lies a contradiction which Lowry never fully articulated but which helped to animate both *Under the Volcano* and the only really important piece of writing which he accomplished before that, namely *Lunar Caustic*. This contradiction is found in the hostile philosophies of two antagonistic figures, the man of action and the man of contemplation. As a man of action Hilliot seeks adventure and the solidarity of working men. As a man of contemplation he wants only solitude, introspection, the underworld of the stokehold. In *Ultramarine*, as in *Lunar Caustic*, these conflicting tendencies are contained within a single individual. In *Under the Volcano* they take on a complex life of their own in the characters of Hugh, a socialist adventurer, and the Consul, a passive cynical spectator of the follies of mankind. For Lowry these two characters represent the poles of human possibility – whether to be actively part of society, fighting to change it, or whether to be outside it altogether as addict, visionary and drop-out.

Lowry's own sensibility was undoubtedly deeply fissured by

21

these antagonistic *Weltanschauungen*. The dust-jacket of the first edition of *Ultramarine* carried a ringing message from its young author: 'I lived through this experience for myself [. . .] if it "rings bells" with anybody else, if one person can feel a stir of fellowship for it . . . I shall have justified myself to myself.' This blurb seems oddly naive, expressing just the kind of gushing feeling which the novel itself places and mocks. The wit and irony of *Ultramarine* explodes ideals of fellowship. As far as Hilliot is concerned, to be sophisticated and authentic is to stand alone, apart from the narrowness of both bourgeoisie *and* proletariat. Lowry himself seems not to have enjoyed his 1927 voyage and he made no lasting friendships with his working-class associates. In *Ultramarine* the sailors are de-humanized, barely visible, mere voices. Hilliot likewise regards the indigenous population of Asia as an alien species, without identity, like insects (a barman typically comes from behind his counter 'like a spider from under his leaf' (*U*, p. 91)).

The 1962 revised edition of the novel contains a clumsy interpolation by Lowry: 'I forgot to mention that there was a war on about half a mashie shot away, it being June, 1927, but that has no part in the story' (*U*, p. 96). The remark is astonishingly casual since the 'war' in question was the Chinese civil war. Lowry sailed into Shanghai not long after Chiang Kai-shek's infamous massacre of local workers in April 1927. It was a turning-point in modern Chinese history, and the turmoil which Lowry witnessed from the harbour marked the collapse of the early revolutionary movement and an historic rupture between the embryonic Chinese Communist Party and the Kuomintang.

All this is absent from *Ultramarine*. The 'Nighttown' chapter makes oriental life seem engagingly surreal; Asia is familiar only as a repository of western capitalist culture, a place of bars, brothels and western movies. Lowry's retrospective comment indicates a disdainful class attitude, the provincialism of which is perfectly summed-up by the golfing metaphor (a mashie is an iron used for medium distances).

The younger Lowry was not quite so prepared to minimize his first-hand experience of events which were to affect the destiny of a quarter of mankind. As his short story 'China' (written in the late 1920s) indicates, Lowry did not so much 'forget' to write about the Chinese revolution as deliberately omit something beyond his understanding. 'China' describes a cricket match between two ship's crews, in a Chinese port. In the distance the civil war is in progress and the thunder of guns can be heard. Upper lips however remain stiff; the cricket match is very 'English'. But the story ends with the narrator returning to his own ship and gazing in horrified disbelief at the cargo which is being unloaded: 'scouting planes, a bomber, a fighting plane, machine guns, anti-aircraft guns, 25 pound bombs, ammunition' (*PAS*, p. 54). The narrator recoils from his involvement in these events, crying out that it was all just a dream, that he wasn't *really* there. China is a place which the narrator cannot understand and does not wish to. It is 'a muddle', 'a queer dream', 'unreal', he doesn't 'believe in China' (*PAS*, p. 49). He is content to leave Shanghai hidden behind a bank of Dickensian fog, distant, opaque and impenetrable.

It comes as something of a surprise, then, to find that within eighteen months of the publication of *Ultramarine* Lowry's fiction was suddenly registering a social-political awareness previously absent. This radical transformation in Lowry's consciousness is signalled in two stories written the following year – a year which was clearly important to Lowry, since he brought it into both titles: 'June 30th, 1934!' and 'Economic Conference, 1934.' The former story is set on the day Hitler organized the massacre of the Brownshirt leaders. A clergyman named (with rather obvious irony) Goodyear travels home on the Paris–London boat train with a fellow Englishman, a veteran of the 1914–18 war. Arriving back in England, Goodyear buys the *Star* and is reassured by its anodyne account of events in Nazi Germany. Later, Goodyear falls asleep and his anxieties about another European war rise terrifyingly to the surface. The story ends on a note of expressionistic nightmare with Goodyear and his companion plunging helplessly towards the holocaust to come, passive victims of history.

'Economic Conference, 1934' replays the meetings of international statesmen as farce. Bill (an American) and Bill (a Londoner) get drunker and drunker in a room filled with absurd relics of English bourgeois culture. Finally they smash up the room. Their debauch is clearly meant to evoke the madness of the world at large, and there are references to reparations, fascism, war debts, the Far East crisis, the Polish corridor and numerous other explosive issues of the day.

Lowry's work was now moving towards the mainstream and his 1930s stories, as well as the earliest surviving drafts of *Under the Volcano*, bear that classic feature of much contemporary writing, the sense 'of the violation of intimate private occasions, by politics, by war, by Europe, by the noises of history'.[9] In 'Inside the Whale' (1940) George Orwell noted how by 1934–5 it was considered eccentric in literary circles not to be more or less left-wing in politics and how the Communist Party had an almost irresistible fascination for young writers. Lowry did not move in literary circles, nor did he join the CP. However, in 1934 he did marry Jan Gabrial, a young Jewish American who may have been a Party member and who certainly took a keen interest in left-wing politics and proletarian fiction. She apparently contributed to left-wing magazines and was trying to write a novel about Hungarian coalminers. The marriage was not a success, and 'Hotel Room in Chartres' (1934) records its fractious early days. Jan Gabrial herself later responded with her own story, 'Not With a Bang', giving the woman's point of view. She seems to have been an independent-minded feminist who singlehandedly raised Lowry's consciousness, converting him to a loosely socialist viewpoint.

Her influence shows up in *Lunar Caustic*,[10] a novella of fifty pages which diagnoses the malady of the 1930s (Auden's 'low, dishonest decade') with extraordinary intensity and conviction. To turn to *Lunar Caustic* after *Ultramarine* is to encounter a profound change in Lowry's sensibility and artistic technique. It is a work which lacks his characteristic humour and verbal invention. An English drunkard named Plantagenet wakes up in a psychiatric hospital after going on a bender through the bars of New York. Here, he encounters a timeless world of suffering and violence which bears a curious resemblance to the timebound world outside. Plantagenet feels that he has 'voyaged downward to the foul core of his world; here was the true meaning underneath all the loud inflamed words, the squealing headlines, the arrogant years' (*PAS*, p. 279). He has arrived at the modern heart of darkness, and the sickness and madness which he discovers there serve as metaphors for the state of western civilization. Outside, in the sane world, it is 1936. The Spanish civil war has just broken out; a barber is on trial for the murder of his bride; Roosevelt is making speeches attacking warmongers. As the fable about the baby elephant suggests, the self-styled 'sane' world is one of cruelty and barbarism, distorting and severing all natural relations. It is, Plantagenet perceives,

> a mischievous world over which merely more subtle lunatics exerted almost supreme hegemony, where neurotic behaviour was the rule, and there was nothing but hypocrisy to answer the flames of evil, which might be the flames of judgement, which were already scorching nearer and nearer. (p. 279)

The apocalyptic note sounded here is echoed elsewhere in the text. The sudden, catastrophic destruction of Pompeii is recalled. An old man remembers the great European war of 1870, the last one before the First World War. There is an oblique allusion to that war also in the story of the barge: 'In 1914 she was loaded with fine coals, but the rope snapped, she drifted with the current, and most of the coal is at the bottom now. The rest is buried here and the barge is smashed, broken' (*PAS*, p. 275). In the era of fascism Lowry makes it clear that western civilization is once again 'drifting with the current.' Plantagenet imagines he sees the corpse of a man on the old barge. It is both himself and Europe. Maritime imagery runs through the narrative. There are references to two famous doomed ships, the *Titanic* and Ahab's *Pequod*. Plantagenet remembers the *Providence*, a paddle-steamer associated with the collapse of his marriage. He claims his name is Lawhill, after a windjammer which survived numerous disasters. The identification is false; Plantagenet's real name – that of a royal house divided against itself – is more appropriate. At the end his mind resembles a sinking ship, 'turning over with disunion of hull and masts uprooted' (*PAS*, p. 304).

In the ward Plantagenet feels a kinship with three inmates in particular. There is Garry, a 14-year-old who compulsively tells short lyrical stories with catastrophic endings, and his companion Mr Kalowsky, an old Jewish refugee. There is also Battle, a burly Negro. The first two seem innocent, sympathetic characters, in contrast to Battle, whose personality has been twisted out of all recognition. Battle, a hyperactive, belligerent shell of a man, is an ex-ship's fireman. As such he represents someone who has followed the tendencies of the *poète maudit* to their logical culmination – lunacy.

Each of these three characters represents facets of Plantagenet's own personality taken to grotesque and distressing extremes. Like Garry, Plantagenet is (as the implied author of *Lunar Caustic*) a maker of fictions, a prophet who sees 'disaster encompassing not only himself but the hospital, this land, the whole world' (*PAS*, p. 293). Like Kalowsky, he is rootless and dispossessed, a modern Wandering Jew. Like Battle, who attempts incoherent semaphore messages to an unwatching world, he cannot communicate meaningfully with other people.

Plantagenet's response to the nightmare world of 1936 is ambivalent. The most radical voice to be heard in *Lunar Caustic* is Kalowsky's:

> If the workers will wake up and buy brains I won't need to go to the hospital! Give the patients nicer to eat! Listen, once they pulled three teeth out of me, out of my mouth. That's the capitalist system. (*PAS*, p. 301)

Plantagenet shows some signs of wanting to change the system. He complains that the nurses are overworked and underpaid and that one nurse has to sell blood to top up his income. He criticizes the hospital routine for encouraging the apathy and passivity of the patients. He protests about the poor standards of hygiene and cleanliness in the hospital. He accuses the obtuse and paternalistic Dr Claggart of being resigned to the system and of merely adjusting others to it. At the end Plantagenet despondently stares out from the hospital and has a prophetic vision of the approaching Second World War. The deluge is coming and no one but himself can see it; down below people are asleep in the park, 'content still in an eighteenth-century day' (*PAS*, p. 297).

It is not Plantagenet who will wake them. Released to the streets he reverts to liquor and escapism: 'When so much suffering existed, what else could a man do?' (*PAS*, p. 305) He dreams of an heroic sacrifice which will save mankind, but the only gesture which he proves capable of is angrily to hurl his whisky bottle at an obscene sketch on a wall. His act of misdirected, futile violence makes him finally one with the three inmates he has left behind. He retires into escapist darkness, a passive victim of history rather than an active transformer of it.

This ambivalence in Plantagenet's character partly reflects a textual instability. *Lunar Caustic* is a posthumous amalgam of 'The Last Address' and 'Swinging the Maelstrom', two separate but overlapping stories which Lowry worked on between 1935 and 1941. In the second story there is a suggestion that the hero will master his neuroses and make the positive gesture of joining the crew of a Loyalist ship bound for the Spanish civil war. Lowry's uncertainly about whether or not to end on a negative or positive note resembles F. Scott Fitzgerald's indecision about converting Dick Diver to Communism at the close of *Tender is the Night* (1939). The editors, like Fitzgerald, decided against a political ending. The older Lowry would probably have endorsed their choice. In 1952 he considered joining the two stories under the title which was eventually used, explaining that 'lunar caustic' was a name for silver nitrate, once used to try and cure syphilis – 'it might stand symbolically for any imperfect or abortive cure, for example of alcoholism'.[11]

In 1936 Lowry and Jan Gabrial drifted down to Mexico. The United States was perhaps beginning to pall for him. He had failed to obtain work in Hollywood. Mexico promised an exotic escape route, somewhere the Lowrys could go in order to try and repair their shattered marriage. It also had the practical advantage of being a cheap country to live in. In Mexico Lowry found a landscape of snowcapped volcanoes, ravines, tropical lushness and human squalor. His sensibility was immediately engaged. Here his wife left him and he was thrown in jail, 'not for being drunk, but for an expression of genuine political opinion in what was a pro-Franco joint' (*DAG*, p. 123). The experience of imprisonment 'had been the end of his little pilgrimage to free humanity' (*DAG*, p. 221). These events seem to have created in Lowry a sense both of persecution and of emotional identity with the downtrodden and outcast of society. *Under the Volcano* is the only novel of Lowry's which contains a large cast of convincingly realized proletarian characters. As Andrew J. Pottinger points out, the novel tentatively suggests 'that the only characters who can see straight, who are not alienated from their fellow men by distrust, are the ordinary Mexican people "of indeterminate class" whom, significantly, "the Consul hated to look at."'[12]

After his wife left him Lowry became the drinking partner of Juan Márquez, a native Mexican. Mexico at this time was undergoing political crisis and destabilization, and Márquez, evidently a political activist and supporter of the Mexican Revolution, educated him in local politics. It was during this phase of the novelist's life that he quarrelled with his old friend, Conrad Aiken. Aiken believed that Lowry had drifted towards Communism; Lowry brusquely wrote that he 'no longer thought of the pro-fascist Conrad as a friend'.[13] (In a letter to *The Times Literary Supplement*, 16 February 1967, Aiken claimed that 'the entire argument, between the Consul and the other, about Marxism in *Under the Volcano* was a verbatim report of an argument between Malcolm and myself, with the positions reversed: what the Consul says, I said.')

Later, Lowry explained that *Under the Volcano* was 'quite definitely on one plane of political parable – indeed it started off as such' (*SL*, p. 199). But though Lowry began writing his masterpiece with politics uppermost in his mind, he spent ten years writing it. During those ten years his sensibility underwent considerable change. After 1938 Lowry never saw Jan or Márquez again. Their waning influence upon him must have been further dissipated by the Nazi-Soviet pact of the following year, which disgusted and demoralized many on the Left.

In 1939 Lowry met the woman who was to become his second wife and moved north, to Vancouver. Margerie Bonner was an ex-child-star of Hollywood's silent movie days. Her interests were astronomy and detective novels, not socialist politics. Lowry originally entered Canada on legal advice, in order to avoid Jan Gabrial's divorce action. However, when he tried to cross back into the USA he was refused entry because of drunkenness. Margerie immediately abandoned California and went up to Vancouver to join Lowry. They were married in that city the following year. After the war broke out they retreated to the squatter settlement at Dollarton, some miles east of Vancouver.

The temper of Lowry's expatriation had always been curiously oblique and marginal. His disposition had always been to operate on the cultural fringes and at Dollarton this tendency was taken to a new extreme. In the past Lowry's major cultural bond had been with Conrad Aiken; in Canada his only important literary friendship was with the poet and novelist Earle Birney. At Dollarton Lowry became – and remained for the rest of his career – an isolated figure, increasingly out of touch with contemporary writing (though not with contemporary criticism). At Dollarton Lowry fell under the influence of Charles Stansfeld-Jones, a former member of Aleister Crowley's 'Hermetic Students of the Golden Dawn'. Soon Lowry had become fascinated by black magic and the occult. His recoil from his erstwhile radicalism could not have been more extreme, and soon he was writing jokey letters to Aiken announcing that he had 'at last join[ed] the ranks of the petty bourgeoisie' (SL, p. 51). The contradictory impulses of the years 1936–44 proved of enormous value in animating the complex fictional world of his masterpiece. Above all, Lowry's experiences of Mexico enabled him to connect the destiny of the romantic outsider to contemporary history and make it seem exemplary.

2

'UNDER THE VOLCANO': MODERNISM AND THE SELF

'You have studied the story more exactly and for a longer time than I have,' said K. They were both silent for a little while. Then K. said: 'So you think the man was not deluded?' 'Don't misunderstand me,' said the priest, 'I am only showing you the various opinions concerning that point. You must not pay too much attention to them. The scriptures are unalterable and the comments often enough merely express the commentator's bewilderment.' (Franz Kafka, *The Trial*)

Every novel is an ideal plane inserted into the realm of reality. (Jorge Luis Borges, 'Partial Magic in the Quixote')

To read *Under the Volcano* is to plunge into a strange, unfamiliar, perplexing fictional terrain. The book is set in Mexico, a land which Lowry renders as a kind of Alice-in-Wonderland world, irrational, hallucinatory, a domain of dreams and nightmares. It is a world peopled by odd, dreamlike figures – old women who keep chickens under their dresses, men without noses, figures who go by such names as 'The Elephant' or 'A Few Fleas'. Lowry magnifies this atmosphere of sinister enchantment by setting the action of his novel on the Day of the Dead, a weird, surreal, even raucous Mexican festival of pagan origins. On this day families picnic in cemeteries and decorate the graves of their loved ones, children play with toy skeletons, bread and sweets in the shape of skulls are sold and eaten, and people dress up as skeletons. Against the gigantism of the landscape and the sheer theatricality of Mexico Lowry's European and American characters move like somnambulists, bearing the burden of their cultures and their pasts.

But Lowry's Mexico is also real. The novel is situated at a precise moment in history (albeit now almost half a century away from us) and there is a close attention to domestic and international politics of the period. The multifarious historical, geographical and cultural citations of Lowry's encyclopedic narrative make the novel difficult to place; critical estimates and interpretations vary wildly. *Under the Volcano* is a curiously Janus-faced novel in which the logic of dreams and history, of the unconscious and the real, constantly intermingle. Echoing Borges' comments on *Don Quixote*, we might say that Lowry 'takes pleasure in confusing the objective and the subjective, the world of the reader and the world of the book.'[14] The language in which the novel is written – English – signifies the discourse of custom, familiarity, reason, 'civilization' perhaps. But language, the very medium of communication, becomes unstable. Meaning begins to blur, sometimes comically. The abbreviated Spanish personal pronoun 'Vd!' ('you!') takes on an altogether different meaning to English eyes. In Lowry's novel English is constantly impinged upon by other languages – French, Latin, German, but chiefly Mexican Spanish and pidgin English. These create a kind of sub-text in the narrative, signifying the alien, the unfamiliar, the dark realms of the unconscious. (*Under the Volcano* must be the only British novel ever published which ends with three sentences in Spanish.)

It is noticeable that critics have had great difficulty in even defining, in a single sentence, what the novel is *about*. Sherrill Grace calls it 'a book about failure and *acedia*';[15] Douglas Day settles for 'the greatest religious novel of this century';[16] Roger Bromley interprets it as 'a reading of the cultural-political situation of the intellectual in the 1930s'.[17] The fertility and complexity of Lowry's narrative make all singleminded definitions and readings of *Under the Volcano* inevitably seem partial and inadequate.

Although Lowry's masterpiece signals its contemporaneity

by the ways in which (to adapt Roland Barthes) it 'make[s] the reader no longer a consumer, but a producer of the text',[18] *Under the Volcano* nevertheless possesses some old-fashioned virtues. It has a beginning, a middle and an end (strictly speaking, two beginnings, a middle and two endings). The pained relations of the four central characters and the Consul's slow slide to death give the book a powerful narrative drive. There is a complicated plot, involving both the tangled lives of the leading characters and the murder of an Indian bank messenger. Above all, there is Lowry's great tragic creation, Geoffrey Firmin, 'the Consul'. Since Lowry's statement that characterization in *Under the Volcano* is 'virtually nonexistent' (*SL*, p. 60) has been approvingly quoted *ad nauseam* it is worth adding that Lowry was talking nonsense (an excusable trait in a novelist desperately trying to convince someone to publish his manuscript). Though there is no authoritative, omniscient authorial assessment of the four leading characters they are otherwise established with all the solidity of nineteenth-century realism. We witness their behaviour, learn their thoughts, discover their ages and backgrounds; their physiognomies are palpable, their corporeity not in doubt. There are also a host of minor characters – Dr Vigil, the Englishman with the Trinity tie, Señora Gregorio, Mr Quincey, the *pelado*, Cervantes, the police chiefs – who are all convincingly fleshed-out and who help to animate and deepen the book. This cast of characters is far from being one of disembodied ciphers – like the spectral creatures of *Gravity's Rainbow* or the 'voices' of Lowry's own late experimentalist work, 'Through the Panama'.

The baleful influence of Lowry's famous letter to Jonathan Cape (*SL*, pp. 57–88) has led to another critical commonplace about *Under the Volcano*, namely that 'There is almost no "story", no external action'.[19] This is simply not true. Lowry's dense, difficult prose ought not to obscure the fact that the novel's power springs primarily from its telling of a story. While wishing to convey a distinctly modern sense of dislocation and relativism, Lowry was not prepared to renounce a naturalistic base to his fiction. The readability of *Under the Volcano* lies in its dramatization of conflicting desires and ambitions – of Geoffrey Firmin's yearning for death and oblivion, his smouldering sense of sexual betrayal, the efforts of Yvonne to draw him back into a loving relationship, and the disastrous presence of her ex-lovers, Hugh and M. Laruelle. This domestic situation takes on a wider perspective as Hugh, Yvonne and Geoffrey become entangled in local politics, an involvement which culminates in the Consul's murder by a fascist vigilante.

The three secondary characters each challenge the Consul's slow suicide through drink and put forward values which (in their eyes) make life worth living. Laruelle is a film director and a collector of Mexican artefacts. He inhabits a stylized studio, lives a promiscuous, sensual, bohemian existence, and represents (in a somewhat corrupt and decadent form) the claims of art. Hugh on the other hand is a committed radical journalist, a member of the *Federación Anarquista Ibérica*. He believes in social change and the brotherhood of man. Yvonne offers love, a meaningful human relationship, the possibility of stability and a home. The Consul rejects each of these possibilities. He is seriously attracted only to what Yvonne offers, but the presence of Laruelle and Hugh provides a searing reminder of her sexual infidelities and forms a major impediment to their chances of reconciliation.

We might wonder why, when two volcanoes dominate the action of the novel, Lowry's title refers only to one volcano. The answer, I think, is that Lowry was alluding to Thomas Hardy's *Under the Greenwood Tree*, deliberately playing off his own immensely complex fictional world against Hardy's simple account of English rural life. *Under the Greenwood Tree* (1872) was Hardy's second published novel, perhaps his slightest, certainly his least sensational. Its overriding quality is innocence – both technical and thematic. It is a simple village love story, about three rivals for the hand of Fancy Day, a young school-teacher. Hardy's novel ends with a wedding feast, literally 'under the greenwood tree' – a massive, ancient tree signifying stability, continuity, fertility.

The volcano of Lowry's title signifies an exactly opposite reality, of hidden forces bubbling beneath the surface, threatening to burst out and destroy. Lowry's Mexico is the dark, terrifying inverse of Hardy's quiet, English and-they-all-lived-happily-ever-after pastoral. He explained that in *Under the Volcano* the 'Tree of Life' (an image derived from the Jewish Cabbala) is upside-down:

> The Cabbala is used for poetic ends because it represents Man's spiritual aspirations. The Tree of Life, its emblem, is a kind of complicated ladder whose summit is called Kether, or Light, while somewhere in its midst an abyss opens out. The spiritual domain of the Consul is probably Qliphoth, the world of husks and demons, represented by the Tree of Life turned upside down and governed by Beelzebub, the God of Flies.[20]

Lowry keeps the symbolic example of Hardy's greenwood tree ironically before the reader throughout the novel. The first trees mentioned in chapter 1 are green ones, which might seem affirmative (healthy, fertile) but are immediately qualified: 'green trees *shot* by evening sunlight might have been *weeping* willows' (*UTV*, p. 9; p. 15; my italics). A few sentences later there are further suggestions that Mexico is a place of sudden transformation and death: 'How continually, how startlingly, the landscape changed! Now the fields were full of stones: there was a row of dead trees' (*UTV*, p. 9; p. 15). Later Laruelle notices trees which look as if they are covered in coal dust, an image perhaps implying the sulphurous proximity of the infernal regions.

The comparison with Hardy's novel reappears in the main body of the novel. Chapter 2 begins in the town square, a location which contains a little scribe 'under a tree [. . .] crashing away on a giant typewriter' (*UTV*, p. 53; p. 58) – Lowry's ironic portrait of himself and his epic narrative. The square also contains an equestrian statue, 'under the nutant trees' (*UTV*, p. 44; p. 49). The trees droop, signifying aridity, barrenness, the drying-up of life. In the following chapter the Consul attempts intercourse with Yvonne but is impotent. Hardy's greenwood tree is associated with celebration, marriage, social stability and continuity. In the Consul's eyes such virtues are bourgeois, false, repellent. The description of Tlaxcala in the tourist brochure reiterates this basic theme of

Lowry's novel. The city synthesizes the bourgeois virtues, being distinguished by 'pleasant appearances, straight streets, archaic buildings, neat fine climate, efficient public electric light, and up to date Hotel for tourists' (*sic*) (*UTV*, p. 297; p. 298). But the Tlaxcalans are also regarded as Mexico's traitors (they formed an alliance with the Spaniards and helped to destroy the Aztec empire). It is therefore appropriate that the Central Park should turn out to be symbolically covered by 'stricken in years trees, ash-trees being the majority' (*UTV*, p. 297; p. 298). Hugh, Yvonne and Laruelle are, like the Tlaxcalans, betrayers, and the cuckolded Consul refuses to take part in their charade of bourgeois good behaviour.

Whereas *Under the Greenwood Tree* ends in a wood that is tranquil and life-affirming, the trees in the wood at the close of *Under the Volcano* are possessed, alive with expressionistic fury. The trees have almost the last word in the novel, 'as though [. . .] crowding nearer, huddled together, closing over [the Consul], pitying' (*UTV*, p. 375; p. 376). The non-human world substitutes for the human relationships which are absent from the Consul's life and which are still lacking when he goes to his lonely death.

*

In its most immediate human aspect *Under the Volcano* is about the aftermath of a divorce. When Yvonne returns the Consul regards her with distrust and makes sarcastic jokes about being Consul to Cuckoldshaven. At Laruelle's house they embrace, but the Consul gazes over her head, thinks of saying that he loves her but can never forgive her deeply enough, and finally mutters cryptically about his heart, disengaging himself from her arms and going to join the others. Their last opportunity for reconciliation occurs while they sit alone at the Arena Tomalín. Yvonne gushes about the simple life; the Consul replies with a sad, world-weary irony. The ellipses in his dialogue point to the vacuum at the heart of their relationship. Their conversation, apparently about together-ness and intimacy, becomes just another illustration of their distance from each other. Yvonne's maiden name is Constable, a double-edged name signifying both her desire to 'arrest' the

Consul's fall and the placid English landscapes of Constable the painter.

Yvonne's dream of going off to live with the Consul on a farm is naive and simplistic. Hugh understands this, as well as the Consul: 'One wonders how she will feel the first time she sees someone stick a pig' (*UTV*, p. 182; p. 185). The allusion is to the grotesque, gory pig-sticking scene in *Jude the Obscure*. Yvonne is a scarlet woman with red shoes and a scarlet bag. Upon encountering Hugh she brushes the dirt from her hands, a gesture which signifies (in a rather Bunyanesque fashion) her guilty past.

Yvonne seems to find Hugh's unexpected presence in Quauhnahuac equally as congenial as her ex-husband's. She repeatedly detaches herself from the Consul in order to enjoy Hugh's company. She and Hugh go horseriding, wander off to look at the palace frescoes, explore the fairground, go swimming together, and end the day alone in the woods. Yvonne reveals herself to be disastrously insensitive to the Consul's quietly raging jealousy. His suspicions are perhaps not altogether without foundation. In chapter 11 Hugh decides not to depart that night for Mexico City after all. He buys a symbolically phallic guitar. Yvonne decides it might be nice to get drunk. There are many subliminal suggestions that Hugh and Yvonne are rather enjoying their re-encounter (as when they are each given a menu at the restaurant but prefer to share hers). Until a very late stage in the writing of the novel, chapter 11 was to have ended with Hugh and Yvonne making love under the trees, Yvonne's impressions of rising towards the stars expressive not of death, but of orgasm.

This explosive triangular situation is not improved when they bump into Laruelle, who seizes Yvonne's arm and insists they all come to his house. *Under the Volcano* gives us a post-Freudian view of human relations. Yvonne's suppression of the memory of Laruelle's house in chapter 2 is a classic example of what Freud described in *The Psychopathology of Everyday Life* as the mechanism of forgetting through *aversion*. It is clear that Yvonne is ashamed of her affair with Laruelle and has no wish to renew it. Laruelle is a flashy, pushy, lecherous bachelor, 'as it were impelled by clockwork', with

36

'bold protuberant eyes' (*UTV*, p. 190; p. 194) and an in-gratiating manner. Lowry portrays him, grotesquely, as a kind of walking erect penis, his trousers 'giving the character of an independent tumescence of the lower part of his body', 'the whole of this man, by some curious fiction, reached up to the crown of his perpendicularly raised Panama hat' (*UTV*, p. 190; p. 194). Hugh commits his own revealing Freudian slip when, on first sighting Yvonne, he mistakenly thinks she is nude.

Alcohol cushions the Consul against what he perceives as the hypocrisy and treachery of his wife, his brother and his friend, but it also inflames his neuroses. *Under the Volcano* is, like the scenery described in the tourist brochure, 'suggestive' (*UTV*, p. 297; p. 298), a book full of *double entendre*. It is a novel in which numerous characters strive to keep themselves *erect* (a word repeated on many occasions).

The mysterious Lee Maitland episode at the beginning of chapter 10 mixes a number of symbols derived from dreams analysed by Freud in *The Interpretation of Dreams*. There are obscure indications of past homosexual behaviour on the Consul's part. In his reverie he finds himself on 'the wrong side of the tracks' (*UTV*, p. 282; p. 284), his bouquet (signifying a sexual relationship) 'a failure', perhaps because it is comprised of 'queen's lace' (*UTV*, p. 283; p. 284). This episode is full of oblique and not-so-oblique sexual symbolism, implying a life-time of sexual guilts and anxieties.

Ironically, this reverie is followed by a confrontation be-tween the Consul and a *cock*: 'Cervantes, rising playfully from behind it, greeted him with Tlaxcaltecan pleasure: "Muy fuerte [very hard]. Muy terreebly," he cackled' (*UTV*, p. 286; p. 288). Cervantes produces a menu, offers them all 'Onans' (*UTV*, p. 290; p. 292) and glides in and out of the scene 'carrying his fighting cock' (*UTV*, p. 299; p. 300). These sex-ual innuendoes culminate in the Consul's furious explosion of sexual jealousy in which he echoes the words of both Iago (*Othello*, III. iii) and Leontes (*The Winter's Tale*, I. ii).

At the beginning of the day the Consul has intimations of 'an evil phallic death' (*UTV*, p. 65; p. 70). At its end he thinks he sees an enormous cock, 'clawing and crowing. [. . .] The

Consul snatched a machete. [. . .] Where was that bloody cock? He would chop off its head' (*UTV*, p. 372). Although the narrative encourages many explanations for the Consul's tragedy, at its simplest *Under the Volcano* is a tale of betrayal and sexual rivalries. The Sergeant who shoots the Consul may simply be replying to the provocations of a machete-wielding drunkard, and the story simply one of human miscalculations and misunderstandings.

At the end of the novel the Consul finally recognizes the simple truth which obstructs the possibility of reconciliation: 'he wanted Yvonne and did not want her' (*UTV*, p. 347; p. 348). The ravine which splits the landscape symbolizes *contradiction*, that which cannot be bridged or resolved, and the Consul's irreconcilable attitude to Yvonne is but one of a host of contradictions in *Under the Volcano*. The novel begins with the word 'Two' and ends with the word 'ravine'. Dualism, contradiction, cleavage are fundamental to the novel's structure and fictional world.[21] The epigraphs themselves are contradictory and irreconcilable, pointing in opposite directions, damnation or salvation.

The plot of *Under the Volcano* is crammed with contradictions and ambiguities. The causes of Geoffrey Firmin's drinking and the circumstances of his death are never clearly explained. *Under the Volcano* narrates the last twelve hours in the lives of Yvonne and the Consul, but there are many riddles in the day's events. Yvonne returns to the husband she has lately divorced on information supplied by Louis, a mysterious figure never properly identified. Outside the bar where the Consul has been drinking they encounter a man with dark glasses and a man with a shade, whom the Consul seems mysteriously to know. On their way to the Calle Nicaragua they pass M. Laruelle's house, at which a peon is gazing curiously. Back at his house the Consul receives an unexplained trunk call from someone called Tom. Later, at the Salón Ofélia, Firmin drunkenly recalls an enigmatic woman named Lee Maitland and a Negro bookie, Mr Quattras. Numerous episodes like these contribute to the novel's atmosphere of menace and mystery. They are all open to explanation, but the narrative declines to privilege any particular interpretation. Like the sign it 'certainly seemed to have more question marks than it should have' (*UTV*, p. 129; p. 133).

In his polemical essay, 'Situation of the Writer in 1947', Sartre asserted that contemporary writers had, since 1940, found themselves 'in the midst of a cyclone':

> Whereas our predecessors thought that they could keep themselves outside history and that they had soared to heights from which they could judge events as they really were, circumstances have plunged us into our time. But since we were in it, how could we see it as a whole? Since we were *situated*, the only novels we could dream of were novels of *situation*, without internal narrators or all-knowing witnesses. In short . . . we had to people our books with minds that were half lucid and half overcast, some of which we might consider with more sympathy than others, but none of which would have a privileged point of view either upon the event or upon itself. We had to present creatures whose reality would be the tangled and contradictory tissue of each one's evaluation of all the other characters – himself included – and the evaluation by all the others of himself, *and who could never decide from within whether the changes of their destinies came from their own efforts, from their own faults, or from the course of the universe.*
>
> Finally, we had to leave doubts, expectations, and the unachieved throughout our works, leaving it up to the reader to conjecture for himself by giving him the feeling, without giving him or letting him guess our feeling, that his view of the plot and the characters was merely one among many others. (final italics mine)[22]

All this is extraordinarily pertinent to *Under the Volcano*, for this is exactly what Lowry does: he puts the reader into the situation of sharing the uncertainties and doubts of the four leading characters.

Chapter 1 (set in 1939, one year after the events which follow) gives us Laruelle's speculations about the Consul's life, a retrospective view of Firmin's tragedy which is full of uncertainties. The technique resembles that of a novel by Conrad. We first learn about the Consul as a legendary figure, the subject of reminiscence long after his death. He was, we learn, a diplomat, a hopeless drunk, a man embroiled by catastrophe. He may have been a murderer, a black-magician, a war hero, perhaps a spy. At one point Laruelle even caustically compares him to Lord Jim, and as in *Lord Jim* (to quote an anonymous reviewer in the *Daily News*, 14 December 1900), 'before the story has taken hold of the reader, he feels as though wandering in a morass of wonderful language and incomprehensible events'. Laruelle introduces the tragedy, but he does so in a vague, uncertain way. Words like 'obscure', 'apparently', 'perhaps' and 'mysteriously' crop up frequently, creating a sense of doubt, uncertainty and expectation. But the flashback to 1938 which begins in chapter 2 and stretches to the end of the novel fails to dissolve these obscurities.

Lowry emphasizes the limited perceptions of his characters. In the opening scene in the Bella Vista bar, Yvonne enters 'silently, blinking, myopic' (*UTV*, p. 45; p. 49); the Consul takes some time before he sees her, 'peering shortsightedly about him before recognizing her, standing there, a little blurred probably' (*UTV*, p. 46; p. 51). When Laruelle appears on the scene he consistently and comically misrepresents Hugh as 'Hugues', 'Hugh' and 'Hughes'. *Under the Volcano* is a novel in which identities are confused and perceptions are inadequate, partial or mistaken. Hugh is dressed in borrowed clothes (the Consul's); Yvonne seems not to be dressed in any at all. In a marvellous comic scene the Consul encounters and exposes an Englishman wearing, without justification, a Trinity tie. The *pelado* wears a crucifix, but is predatory and evil. The vigilantes confuse the Consul's identity with Hugh's. The Consul mistakenly perceives the Chief of Rostrums as friendly ('obviously he was a good fellow' (p. 356; p. 357)) but he is the one who murders the Consul, not the sinister Sanabrio or the evil-looking Zuzugoitea. The novel is one in which mistranslations are frequent. Signs are misread, actions misinterpreted. When Yvonne complacently thinks that 'the poor Indian was obviously being taken care of' (p. 256; p. 258) Lowry signals her myopia. The Indian is indeed 'being taken care of' but scarcely in the sense Yvonne means. The Consul hums lines from J. W. Turner's much anthologized (and saccharine) poem

'Romance'. Significantly, he misquotes it (p. 64; p. 69). The poem actually has a sinister application to *Under the Volcano*. The 'golden land' of Mexico takes the Consul's speech away *literally*, by killing him. The contradictions of the novel cannot be resolved; the *barranca* cannot be bridged. In the end contradiction destroys the Consul; the void swallows and silences him.

In this sense we can say that *Under the Volcano* is an experimental novel compellingly aware both of the modern psychic and political condition, in a way that many modernist novels are not. Its mediation of inner and outer disorder and anarchy gives it a specifically mid-twentieth-century texture. What Lowry achieves is a kind of expressionist modernism. *Under the Volcano* powerfully transmits the classic expressionist sense of psychic extremity distorting and transfiguring the everyday world. The Consul's dying scream evokes that *locus classicus* of the expressionist vision, Edvard Munch's *The Scream* (1893), a painting Lowry made a sketch of and almost certainly saw on his visit to Oslo in 1930. This last inarticulate sound which the Consul utters before his death expresses an alienation from humanity and the universe, rippling outwards and returning, an agonizing solitude made tangible and terrifying. Lowry's characteristic irony is absent from the closing lines of the novel. There can be little doubt that *Under the Volcano* is, for all its comic aspects, a major modern tragedy, exciting both pity and terror, its final declamatory words a vehement admonition intended to touch the reader deeply. What makes the novel so unusual in modern writing is the manner in which Lowry succeeds in *situating* his hero's *Angst*. The novel is both inward and outward-looking; the tragically enmeshed self is unable to extricate itself from the equally pressing entanglements of politics and history.

3

'UNDER THE VOLCANO': MODERNISM AND FORM

A novel does not assert anything; a novel searches and poses questions. . . . When Don Quixote went out into the world, that world turned into a mystery before his eyes. That is the legacy of the first European novel to the entire subsequent history of the novel. (Milan Kundera, Afterword to *The Book of Laughter and Forgetting*)

One likes to recall that the difference between the comic side of things, and their cosmic side, depends upon one sibilant. (Vladimir Nabokov, *Nikolai Gogol*)

'A civilization', Yeats wrote, 'is a struggle to keep self-control, and in this it is like some great tragic person.'[23] In *Lunar Caustic* Lowry had portrayed four characters whose derangement was intended as an expression of the malaise of civilization; *Under the Volcano* repeats this formula, switching the action from New York in 1936 to a fictional town in Mexico in the autumn of 1938. Lowry's novel is set on a single day, and in this it bears some resemblance to Joyce's *Ulysses* (1922) and Virginia Woolf's *Mrs Dalloway* (1925).

Sartre proclaimed the importance of Joyce's example to post-war writers, arguing that faced by the urgent imperatives of modern history the great technical problem was 'to find an orchestration of consciousness which may permit [the writer] to render the multi-dimensionality of the event.'[24]Twentieth-century history actually plays little part in *Ulysses*. Joyce (who wrote his novel between 1914 and 1921) was intent on memorializing Edwardian Dublin on 16 June 1904, and neither the outbreak of war in 1914 nor the 1916 Easter Rising (which resulted in the destruction of Dublin's city centre) deflected him from that task. Despite its experimentalism *Ulysses* now seems like the last Victorian novel, an exhaustive portrait of a provincial backwater expressing little sense of evil or violence. (Kafka's vision of city life as nightmarish, threatening, void of coherence, is arguably very much more modern than Joyce's.)

In *Mrs Dalloway* and *Under the Volcano* we witness the forces of modern history beginning to rupture the liberal-humanist values which Joyce chose to celebrate. Woolf's novel, which is set on a June day in 1923, takes us to the heart of British society at a specific historical moment and shows us the moral disintegration of its ruling class. Clarissa Dalloway's Westminster society is one where people 'solidify young'[25] and become dull, reactionary, mired in convention. (Woolf originally conceived that Mrs Dalloway's response to this bloodless high Tory society should be suicide.) It is a class which has lost the will to govern. The signs of its passing are indicated on the margins: the spectre of Labour rule, rebellion in India. The strokes of Big Ben which sound through the novel seem to be tolling its doom.

As social prophecy *Mrs Dalloway* proved to be wide of the mark. One year after its publication the outcome of the General Strike showed that the Richard Dalloways were still very much in control. Stasis, stagnation, insularity remained the order of the day. A dozen years later, George Orwell, returning from the Spanish civil war, grumbled that England was still a place where it was difficult

> to believe that anything is really happening anywhere. Earthquakes in Japan, famines in China, revolutions in Mexico? Don't worry, the milk will be on the doorstep tomorrow morning, the *New Statesman* will come out on Friday. [. . .] it was still the England I had known in my childhood [. . .] the men in bowler hats, the pigeons in Trafalgar Square, the red buses, the blue policemen – all sleeping the deep, deep

sleep of England, from which I sometimes fear that we shall never wake till we are jerked out of it by the roar of bombs.[26]

Lowry possibly had this passage in mind in the scene where Hugh hears the Consul's snores 'wafted to his ears: the muted voice of England long asleep' (*UTV*, p. 98; p. 102). The Consul *is*, to an extent, England, and the contemporary historical context forms an inescapable part of his decline.

Lowry situates the main action of the novel on 2 November 1938, shortly after the Munich agreement was signed. The Spanish civil war was then in its closing stages and provides a constant reference point in the novel. There are references to Hitler, Stalin, Chamberlain, Gandhi, Nehru, the Italian invasion of Abyssinia. More pressingly, there is the domestic crisis of Mexican politics. In 1938 Mexico was torn by political divisions. President Cárdenas, a populist socialist, supported the democratic side in the Spanish civil war, expropriated the holdings of foreign oil companies, gave Trotsky exile, closed down the Casinos, and embarked on a radical programme of land redistribution. In parts of the country law and order had broken down and various fascist and paramilitary groups plotted against the socialist government, including the fanatical Catholic *sinarquistas* and the Union Militar of General Almazán. All these aspects of the political crisis enter into *Under the Volcano*. The Consul's world-weary liberal humanism might not have been out of place in Clarissa Dalloway's drawing room, but in Mexico it is absurdly, even dangerously inappropriate.

Lowry's provincial town in Mexico is (rather like Conrad's Africa but unlike Joyce's Dublin) a reflector of the condition of western civilization, packed with symptoms of decay and impending catastrophe. The opening page of the novel establishes Quauhnahuac's global centrality. In the first paragraph the perspective is an aerial one, reminiscent of the zooming-in-on-a-map technique which featured in the opening sequences of many 1940s movies (a stereotype recently parodied at the start of David Hare's *Saigon − Year of the Cat* (1983)). The second paragraph develops the clichéd cheerfulness of tourist brochures and advertising (the reference to *fifty-seven* cantinas sounds suspiciously like an echo of the famous Heinz advertising slogan). The irony of this is quickly made apparent. These opening pages establish a pervasive mood of entropy and decay. Words like *desolate, ruined, empty, mournful, deserted, melancholy* make the first of their numerous appearances in the text. In a manner which resembles the opening pages of *Nostromo* and *A Passage to India* Lowry establishes the symbolic nature of the terrain.

Quauhnahuac is a waste land, littered with wreckage. Its universality is again stressed: it is a place where you encounter 'every sort of landscape at once' (*UTV*, p. 10; p. 15) – English, French, American, African. It resembles Eden but it is a paradise where the Day of Wrath has arrived. The 'dark swift horses surging up the sky' (*UTV*, p. 10; p. 16) signify the arrival of the four horsemen of the apocalypse; the 'immense archangel, black as thunder' (*UTV*, p. 12; p. 18) seems to have flown straight out of the Book of Revelation.

It is against this landscape that Geoffrey Firmin's tragedy is enacted. Significantly, the four main characters are nationals of major world powers. Laruelle is French, Yvonne American, Hugh and the Consul English (Anglo-Indians, representatives of the British Empire, to be precise). The Consul is an ex-public school, ex-Cambridge man, a member of the governing class. As a former Consul he has directly represented the Crown. His attitude to the dying Indian is one of cautious non-involvement. Like the British government of Neville Chamberlain in the face of aggression by Hitler, Mussolini and Franco he shies away from *doing* anything. Ultimately this attitude rebounds upon him and he finds himself in the same situation as the Indian (or democratic Spain), attacked by fascists, dying alone and friendless.

The political theme is first introduced in chapter 1, from Laruelle's retrospective viewpoint. The Frenchman recalls Señor Bustamente's suggestion that the Consul was actually not really a diplomat at all but a spy – something Laruelle breezily dismisses. But Laruelle reveals himself to be an astonishingly complacent and egocentric individual. His attitude to the outbreak of the Second World War is bland in the extreme: 'He had few emotions about the war, save that it was bad. One side or the other would win. And in either case life would be hard. Though if the Allies lost it would be harder. And in either case one's own battle would go on' (*UTV*, p. 9; p. 15). This demonstrates something more solidly established later in the book: that where anything is concerned Laruelle thinks first of all of himself. He regards the fascist Unión Militar merely as 'tiresome' (*UTV*, p. 23; p. 29). He considers making a version of the Faustus story with someone like Trotsky for its protagonist, which as Bromley points out is 'a false cultural-political synthesis [. . .] Laruelle's intention would transform Trotsky into a cultural fiction and downgrade his real significance.'[27] (There is also the irony that the downfall of the Consul – who at one point is jeeringly identified as Trotsky because of his beard – can be seen as precisely the sort of Faustian tragedy Laruelle envisages, though the Frenchman seems blind to this.) When Laruelle reveals that Sr Bustamente seemed half-convinced that he had been taken in about the Consul's identity it is clear that Sr Bustamente may well be right. Later in the book there is plenty of evidence that the Consul may well be under surveillance, and if he gave the impression 'of a man living in continual terror of his life' (*UTV*, p. 30; p. 36) we can only recall (as Laruelle does not) that he was indeed murdered by the political police. (There is also the question of the Consul's relationship with Señora Gregorio, who, we are cryptically told, 'had had some difficult explanations to make' (*UTV*, p. 31; p. 37).)

The Consul actually seems remarkably well-informed about local politics. At Laruelle's house the names of his murderer's accomplices jump out of the telephone directory at him, a coincidence which is nowhere explained. He points out one of the local 'fascist joints' (*UTV*, p. 234; p. 236) to Hugh, and tries to tell him (Hugh is deep in conversation with Yvonne and doesn't hear) that the Farolito is a local Nazi headquarters. Later, Hugh explains to Yvonne that the dying Indian may have been a messenger for the socialist government's Ejidal bank, but concludes (wrongly) that the fascists 'don't [. . .] have any hold here to speak of' (*UTV*, p. 298; p. 300).

The murder of Geoffrey Firmin is ambiguous and open to a variety of interpretations. The Consul sees the deputies as 'phantoms of himself' (*UTV*, p. 362), an explanation accepted by many critics. There are other constructions which we can put upon the episode, however. The political sub-plot which runs through the novel prepares us for the possibility that the Consul is indeed a spy, working for the British government against the pro-Axis Unión Militar. The Chief of Rostrums may have a concrete political motive for disposing of him. Or it may be that the fascists have confused Geoffrey's identity with that of his anarchist-card-carrying brother. Or it may simply be that the vigilantes are responding in a typically Mexican fashion to the verbal and physical assaults of the drunken, belligerent Consul.

Mexico still has one of the highest murder rates in the world. Graham Greene, who was in Mexico in 1938, noted how 'Several people had been shot by a police chief in a quarrel – that was the regular feature of a Mexican paper; no day passed without somebody's being assassinated somewhere'.[28]

Under the Volcano counterpoises two basic political positions: to change the world (through socialism or art) or to accept it. Laruelle dreams of making great films and effecting a cultural transformation, but the novel places him as a failure, past his prime.

> Yet in the Earthly Paradise, what had he done? He had made few friends. He had acquired a Mexican mistress with whom he quarrelled, and numerous beautiful Mayan idols he would be unable to take out of the country, and he had –
>
> M. Laruelle wondered if it was going to rain (*UTV*, p. 10; p. 16)

As Laruelle himself dimly perceives, the sum of his achievements simply doesn't bear thinking about. His life is dead; he is merely a consumer, one who acquires objects, both animate and inanimate.

Hugh seems a more commanding figure, troubled by his conscience, haunted by the Spanish civil war, determined to be involved. But he, too, is revealed as inadequate, 'a professional indoor Marxman' (*UTV*, p. 8; p. 10) who for all his talk of fight and engagement takes on nothing more strenuous than the procession of wooden ducks which he shoots at at the fairground. Significantly, he is the Consul's *half*-brother, symbolically incomplete, someone who is to be found 'stretching himself to his full mental height of six foot two (he was five feet eleven)' (*UTV*, p. 104; p. 108). The ideal of revolutionary socialism is represented more convincingly by Hugh's friend, Juan Cerillo. Cerillo is a native Mexican who has fought for Republican Spain and who is working (like the murdered Indian) for the Ejidal bank. Cerillo does not put in an appearance in the novel but remains off-stage, a remote, fleetingly presented ideal in Hugh's mind. He is, importantly, the only character of significance who is not subjected to irony.

The episode involving the dying Indian brings Hugh's concerns to the fore. As a messenger for the Ejidal the Indian provides a concrete example of a man victimized by the forces of fascism and repression. He also represents the condition of contemporary Spain. The Indian's dying word *compañero* ('comrade') was the word of greeting used by the Spanish republicans. The two-hatted *pelado* with the crucifix who steals the Indian's money represents the combined force of Catholic-Francoist reaction, and the two diplomatic cars which speed past are obviously intended to symbolize France and Britain.

Set against Hugh's passionate, intoxicated desire for social transformation is the blithe indifference of Yvonne and the weary cynicism of the Consul. Yvonne is wealthy and rootless, the daughter of an American Consul who later became a failed capitalist. Her background makes her kin with the forces of imperialism and exploitation. She has been brought up by a wealthy uncle with financial interests in South America. Hugh apostrophizes her as the archetypal product of 'centuries of oppression' (*UTV*, p. 187; p. 191). Yvonne is only dimly aware of the shattering changes which Cárdenas is instituting in Mexico:

> 'Isn't it an adorable farm,' Yvonne said. 'I believe it's some government experiment. I'd love to have a farm like that.' (*UTV*, p. 105; p. 108)

Her blindness to the real state of things is pinpointed by her failure either to notice the bloodstained coins in the *pelado*'s hands or to realize their significance. As a perceptive reviewer noted in 1947, 'Yvonne can't stand the sight of blood: it is her flaw, her way of acquiescing in the *de facto*.'[29] (In fact Yvonne turns away not at the sight of blood but at the *suspicion* of it.)

Yvonne's indifference to political reality is symptomatic of her narcissism. She is a worldling, nothing more. (Laruelle's translated Shakespeare points up the ironic difference between 'merry wives' and 'Joyeuses Bourgeoises'.) The Consul's self-absorption is compounded of more complex matter. Despite his fascination with occultism and the realms of the transcendental the Consul has some distinctly earthbound interests which put him, too, among the exploiters of mankind. He has been sued for back wages by one or more of his servants; he owns property; he evidently plays the stock exchange; he refers mysteriously to his 'habit of making money' (*UTV*, p. 82; p. 87). As Stephen Tifft points out, the Consul is not entirely an exemplary figure: 'While [Lowry] encourages the reader to sympathize with the Consul's internal constraints, he also seems to levy a judgement on his paralysis, particularly in the political context.'[30]

The shadow which the Spanish civil war casts over the novel underlines the urgency of the case which Hugh is making, however ineptly, for social change. When the Consul pictures his soul as 'a town ravaged and stricken in the black path of his excess [. . .] the whole town plunged into darkness, where communication is lost, motion mere obstruction, bombs threaten, ideas stampede –' (*UTV*, p. 145; pp. 148–9) Lowry probably intends to evoke the bombing of Guernica. The novel looks ahead to the horrors of the Second World War; Hugh has a monstrous vision of 'children piled up, many hundreds' (*UTV*, p. 248; p. 250), an image echoed at the end by the dying Consul's prophetic glimpse of 'ten million burning bodies' (*UTV*, p. 375; p. 376). The imperatives of the Spanish after-text are solemnly exclamatory, as if time is running out.

Roger Bromley has argued that Lowry is

a writer who probably offers the most searching interrogation of the violence exercised by the symbolic forms of power in Western society since Lawrence. [. . .] At one point in *The*

Fate of the Earth, Jonathan Schell says, 'We deny the truth that is all around us. Indifferent to the future of our kind, we grow indifferent to one another. We drift apart. We grow cold. We drowse our way toward the end of the world. . . .' It is not too pretentious, or fanciful I hope, to suggest that this is at the heart of *Under the Volcano*, the failure of Western society to reproduce itself in forms other than those of tyranny, fissure, and destruction.[31]

This is a salutary contemporary reading which makes *Under the Volcano* relevant to our own time. But I am reminded of Tariq Ali's strictures on *Midnight's Children* (1981).[32] Salman Rushdie has asserted that the multitudinous teeming form of his novel 'is the optimistic counterweight to Saleem's personal tragedy. I do not think that a book written in such a manner can really be called a despairing work.'[33] But, Ali argues, this defence is not totally convincing; there is a streak of pessimism and nihilism in *Midnight's Children* which is inescapable and, of course, understandable as a modern vision. *Under the Volcano* likewise possesses a strong undercurrent of nihilism. The Consul scornfully spurns his brother's socialism:

> Can't you see there's a sort of determinism about the fate of nations? They all seem to get what they deserve in the long run. [. . .] Not so long ago it was poor little defenceless Ethiopia. Before that, poor little defenceless Flanders. To say nothing of course of the poor little defenceless Belgian Congo. And tomorrow it will be poor little defenceless Latvia. Or Finland. Or Piddledeedee. Or even Russia. Read history. Go back a thousand years. What is the use of interfering with its worthless stupid course? (*UTV*, pp. 309–10; p. 311)

There is much in *Under the Volcano* that lends support to the Consul's despairing *Weltanschauung*. Lowry portrays Hugh's grasp of Mexican politics as pathetically obtuse; ironically it is the Consul who seems to know exactly what the local fascists are up to. On the bus it is, revealingly, not Hugh but the Consul who spots that the *pelado* is a thief. In their drunken argument at the restaurant the dice are loaded in the Consul's favour. The angry outburst quoted above is historically prescient. In the year after the Consul's murder Latvia was occupied by the Soviet army. Finland was invaded by the USSR on 30 November 1939. In June 1941 Russia was in turn invaded, by Germany. The Consul, apparently only a self-deluding drunk, actually possesses a clairvoyant insight into the future.

The course of Mexican history, as represented by Lowry, seems to justify the Consul's despair. In the sixteenth century Cortés conquered Mexico with the assistance of his Indian mistress and the treacherous Tlaxcalans. In 1846 the USA declared war and seized half of Mexico. In the 1860s Napoleon III encouraged his ambitious young son the Archduke Maximilian of Austria to accept the crown of Mexico, then betrayed him by withdrawing the troops on which his power rested. Maximilian surrendered to the rebel forces and was shot on the orders of Juarez. His wife, Carlotta, went mad. In 1876 Porfirio Diaz launched a revolution but betrayed his country by handing over the land to foreign owners. (Hugh's reverie about Juan Cerillo in chapter 4 describes this phase of Mexican history; significantly Cerillo's father fought with Huerta but then turned traitor.) By the twentieth century Mexico purported to have a socialist regime but it was one in name only. In 1934 Calles appointed Cardenas as the next puppet president. Cardenas promptly established a power base, expelled Calles from the country and set about putting some of the platitudes of the revolution into practice. The 1938 oil crisis and the conflict between socialists, Communists, fascists and Nazis brings the long history of Mexico's betrayals up to the present time of the novel. *Under the Volcano* seems to suggest that history is merely a perpetual process of betrayal and exploitation, of conquerors and victims.

Hugh, Laruelle and Yvonne are themselves part of this pattern. They have each betrayed the Consul. But the Consul is equally burdened with sexual guilt (the Hell Bunker, Lee Maitland). At the same time as Hugh and Yvonne are becoming drawn into a compromising situation in the woods, the Consul is lured, not unwillingly, into the prostitute's room. In addition all four are citizens and representatives of imperialist nations which have preyed on Mexico, and the Consul is perhaps more involved in exploitation than any of them (his mysterious phone call from Tom implies murky share dealings). Like the *pelado* the Consul is both exploited and exploiting. The last two words spoken to him after he has been shot are *pelado* and *compañero*, signifying the polar extremes of self-absorption and comradeship.

*

Self-absorption, however, is the very condition of the text itself. *Under the Volcano* is curiously self-regarding, both physically, as a book, and as a fiction. Lowry was acutely conscious of the physical appearance of the printed page, advising (for example) in chapter 10, 'some experiment [. . .] with the typesetting such as the occasional use of black letter for the headings juxtaposed with anything from cursive down to diamond type for the rest' (*SL*, p. 82). Each page is a visual feast for the eye. The typography forms an integral part of the meaning of the book. It is often used to indicate distortions or displacements of consciousness. Characteristic devices are paragraphs which end with ellipses, and apostrophes which simply enclose (instead of the expected dialogue) other syntactical figures – a hyphen or a hyphen and a question-mark. These sets of three dots and hyphens point to areas of discourse which are being suppressed (perhaps because they are too painful to be communicated). Spanish syntax is introduced to defamiliarize Lowry's fictional world, the upside-down exclamation marks and questionmarks buttressing the reader's impression of a topsy-turvy Alice-in-Wonderland reality. Italic type (significantly a *sloping* type) indicates the irruption of foreign words into the customary discourse of the novel. The general effect is of a breaking-down and blurring of any single homogenous stable reality.

The narrative has a cyclical structure, in which (like the Quauhnahuac cinema) 'the same features come back over and over again' (*UTV*, p. 110; p. 114). Lowry may have learned something from *Finnegans Wake* (1939), published while he was working on *Under the Volcano*. Like Joyce he sought to create a kind of timeless narrative continuum; at the end of the book the reader is expected to turn back to the first page and begin again. The structural image of the wheel recurs in numerous forms in *Under the Volcano* (the Ferris wheel, the 'infernal' looping-the-loop machine, the madman with an old bicycle tyre, the wheeling planets, the constellations), signifying eternity. Time is imprisoning and inescapable. Lowry stresses the fictionality of his characters. They are figures locked into a larger structure, illusory phantoms endlessly repeating situations over which they have no control. Lowry was fond of 'the Bergsonian idea that the sense of time is merely an inhibition to prevent everything happening at once – brooding upon which it is pretty difficult to avoid some notion of eternal recurrence' (*SL*, p. 200). He used a wide range of hermetic literature (astrology, the Tarot, the Cabbala, and the writings of pop metaphysicians like J. W. Dunne, Charles Fort and P. D. Ouspensky) in establishing the cosmology of his fictional universe.

There are three major spiritual symbols in the novel – the ruined garden, the hellish abyss, and the faraway celestial mountain. The Consul is at the centre of this triangle of possibilities, gazing back at the garden he has made into a Waste Land. As his name (an anagram of 'infirm') implies, he is the modern Fisher King. His sacrifice is necessary in order that the arid land can be made fertile once again. The Consul also possesses some of the attributes of the Magician, the Fool and the Hanged Man in the Tarot pack. He is trapped in a demonic universe in which satanic agents – dogs, scorpions, a malevolent sunflower – are tangibly and terrifyingly present. Lowry's use of numerology reinforces this sense of a meshed, imprisoning world. Quauhnahuac is situated on the nineteenth parallel and the Consul is doomed to die at nineteen hundred hours. When the Consul tries, unsuccessfully, to make a telephone call, the number that jumps out at him is 666, the number of the horned beast in the book of Revelation.

What Lowry called the 'borrowings, echoes, design-governing postures' (*SL*, p. 115) derived from other texts and bodies of knowledge are present in abundance in *Under the Volcano*. The narrative draws upon material as diverse as astronomy, Indian mythology, Mexican history, global geography, music, painting, geomorphology, drama, metaphysics, politics, poetry and other novels. *Under the Volcano* aspires (as other encyclopedic novels do) to be a book of books. It represents itself as a compendium of world literature, recreating the fictions of the past.

A major literary analogue is Dante's *Divine Comedy*. The infernal aspect of Lowry's Mexico is comically signalled by the demon brandishing a pitchfork on the label of Laruelle's bottle of beer. Lowry twice refers to the famous opening lines of the *Inferno*:

> Nel mezzo del cammin di nostra vita
> Mi ritrovai per una selva oscura
>
> (In the middle of our journey of life
> I woke to find myself in a dark wood)

On the first page of the novel we encounter the Hotel Casino de la Selva; later, Hugh half-quotes these lines at the start of chapter 6. There are a number of other allusions to woods, leading up to the real dark wood of chapter 11. Moreover at the close of chapter 1 a bell rings out '*dolente . . . dolore!*' (p. 42; p. 47), echoing the words inscribed above the gates of Dante's hell:

> Per me si va nella città dolente,
> Per me si va nell' etterno dolore
>
> (Through me the way to the city of desolation,
> Through me the way to eternal sorrow)

At the end of the book the Consul is thrown into the abyss, which Hugh, alluding to the Eighth Circle of the *Inferno*, identifies as 'the Malebolge' (p. 100; p. 104). The point of these allusions is to indicate the tormented condition of Lowry's characters as they descend (the first line of chapter 8 is simply: 'Downhill . . .') deeper into their private infernos, towards judgement. Lowry's characters are guilty of many of the failings of Dante's sinners – lust, deception, hypocrisy, theft, hoarding, the sowing of discord. Whereas Dante is guided through hell by the poet Virgil, embodying wisdom and morality, the fallen nature of modern man is signified by the vocation of the Consul's guide, Dr Vigil, a specialist in sexual diseases.

Lowry echoes a great number of other texts, including the Bible, the *Mahabharata*, Marlowe's *Dr Faustus*, Goethe's *Faust*, and Kafka's *The Castle* and *The Trial* in his evocation of the condition of mankind in 1938. Perhaps Lowry's most ambitious 're-telling' was of that other twentieth-century book-of-books, Joyce's *Ulysses*. The relationship between the Consul, Hugh and Yvonne presents many parallels to that of Bloom, Stephen Dedalus and Molly. The Consul's 'Greek e's' (*UTV*, p. 35; p. 41) mirror Bloom's epistolary efforts ('Remember write Greek ees').[34] Like Bloom he talks to a cat, calculates what a sum of money would equal in terms of drinks, quotes *Hamlet*, is pursued by a stray dog, is featured sitting on the toilet and has his identity mistaken by phantasmagoric figures of authority. The list of books in Bloom's library and his budget for the day are both directly imitated in *Under the Volcano*. There are dozens of other allusions and echoes, of which the most audacious is Lowry's ironic echo of Molly's famous reply to Bloom's proposal. Hugh urges Yvonne out of the El Popo back into the dark wood, a suggestion which is partly sexual in motivation: 'Yvonne said yes' (*UTV*, p. 331). But whereas Molly Bloom's last words ('I said yes I will Yes') signify fertility, affirmation, life, Yvonne's 'yes' is almost literally her last word, before her death.

In his decline the Consul relives some of the major myths of western civilization. He is Adam, about to be expelled from Paradise; Christ, the sacrificial scapegoat for man's sins; Dante, journeying through an inferno of the damned; Hamlet, disgusted by human sexuality, paralysed by the knowledge of betrayal; Faustus, due to be cast into hell for abusing his powers. (Although *Under the Volcano* sets out to be a book-of-books it is nevertheless very partial in its sources. Lowry completely passes over the tradition of Richardson, Fielding, Defoe, Jane Austen, Scott, Thackeray, George Eliot; his literary affiliations were fundamentally romantic and modernist. Lowry's sensibility was the opposite of Joyce's. Joyce preferred his mythic voyagers to be 'men of substance and family' as opposed to 'Prometheus, Lucifer and Faust, those bachelors, disobedient sons and brilliant failures.'[35])

There are hints that the Consul is a black magician, an

identification with profound implications for the meaning of the novel:

> Yet who would have ever believed that some obscure man, sitting at the centre of the world in a bathroom, say, thinking solitary miserable thoughts, was authoring their doom. (*UTV*, p. 146; p. 149)

The answer is that the reader is persuaded to believe it. It is important to understand the ways in which Lowry seeks to convince us that the Consul is somehow right to reject the alternatives proposed by the other three, that it is *his* vision of life which is the deepest, the most profound.

In chapter 7 Laruelle bitterly criticizes the Consul for his deviation from normal standards of good behaviour; in chapter 9 Yvonne tries to lure the Consul back to married life; in chapter 10 Hugh puts forward his belief in the brotherhood of man. The Consul spurns each of them and retires once more within himself. When critics consider these moments in the novel they invariably side with the Consul against the other characters. T. Bareham's description of the Consul as 'infinitely the most sensitive and intelligent person in the book'[36] is a fairly typical one.

Partly this is a matter of point-of-view. As Nabokov tartly remarks of a character in *Transparent Things* (1972), 'This Henry Emery Person, our Person's father, might be described as a well-meaning, earnest, dear little man, or as a wretched fraud, depending on the angle of light and position of the observer.'[37] From the intimacy of the Consul's mind the angle of light does not favour the other characters, and almost half the novel is seen through his eyes. But, more crucially, there is an underlying complicity between the narrative and the Consul. Lowry's fictional universe endorses the Consul's intuition of mysterious occult connections at the heart of things. Mexico emerges as a sinister, magical world of uncanny symmetries. The role of the pariah dogs as Faustian familiars or demons is underlined by puns: 'the pariah dog [. . .] appeared familiarly at heel' (*UTV*, p. 66; p. 70); 'It was a pariah dog and disturbingly familiar' (*UTV*, p. 127; p. 131). There are all kinds of odd reverberations in the novel. Dr Vigil's phrase 'progresión a ratos' ['journey from time to time'] (*UTV*, p. 144; p. 148) is echoed by Zuzugoitea's semi-obscene 'Progresión al culo' ['journey to the bottom'] (*UTV*, p. 357; p. 358). The postman's grunt, 'Ei ei ei ei ei ei' (*UTV*, p. 192; p. 196) is echoed by Laruelle's 'Ei ei ei ei' (*UTV*, p. 201; p. 205). Hugh's whinny, '*Wh-wh-wh-wh-wh-wh-wh-wh-wheeee-u*' (*UTV*, p. 106; p. 110) is echoed by Dr Vigil's 'Wheee' (*UTV*, p. 147; p. 151).

Lowry's fictional universe is one which perpetually duplicates and reduplicates itself. Connections are established, but they are sometimes absurd or irrational, more the fabric of a dream world than a naturalistic reality. Lowry explained that his intention was 'to make a noise like music' (*SL*, p. 200) rather than to achieve a consistent realism. The narrative proceeds analogically and the real, historical world of 1938 often seems to crumble away into a dream world.

It is as if the whole novel is actually taking place inside the Consul's mind. The language and values of Hugh, Yvonne and Laruelle tend to express, surreptitiously, the Consul's. Hugh, for example, characterizes Yvonne as the archetypal American female:

> Women of medium height, slenderly built, mostly divorced, passionate but envious of the male – angel to him as he is bright or dark, yet unconscious destructive succubus of his ambitions – American women, with that rather graceful swift way of walking, with the clean scrubbed tanned faces of children, the skin finely textured with a satin sheen, their hair clean and shining as though just washed, and looking like that, but carelessly done, the slim brown hands that do not rock the cradle, the slender feet – how many centuries of oppression have produced them? (*UTV*, p. 187; p. 191)

This is an extraordinary passage which goes to the heart of the narrative's contradictory presentation of Yvonne. Though Lowry tacks on a political motive for Hugh's spasm of revulsion (Yvonne doesn't care who will win the Spanish civil war), it is clear that what really repels him is her ruthless sexuality. Yvonne is both whore and angel, a mixture of experience (passionate, divorced) and childlike innocence, as beautiful and smartly dressed as a model but with revealingly brown

skin. She is a threatening figure with (it is hinted) an indis-
criminate sexual appetite. She spurns the claims of the nuclear
family, since her hands will never 'rock the cradle'. She is also
'envious' of men, though why this should be so is not made
clear, especially since the ways in which she destroys their
ambitions are 'unconscious', and the nature of those ambitions
remains unspecified. It is as if Lowry wanted his heroine to
seem like Nicole in Scott Fitzgerald's *Tender is the Night*, the
destroyer of a man's promising career.

These thoughts are doubly curious coming from Hugh, who,
unlike the furious and disgusted Consul, knows nothing of
Yvonne's affair with Laruelle. Odd, too, is Hugh's particularly
virulent branding of Yvonne as a 'destructive succubus'. This
again highlights the sexual nature of his hostility (a succubus is
a female demon supposed to have sexual intercourse with
sleeping men). The term is a strange one for Hugh to use and
belongs much more with the Consul's occult vocabulary.

Yvonne is the source of three other violent outbursts of
sexual disgust in the novel, and each comes from the Consul:
his reaction to the sight of Laruelle nude, his description of
Yvonne's first husband's lovemaking, and his Shakespearean
jeers at the other two in the restaurant. The passage in fact
seems quite inconsistent with Hugh's character. He is unaware
of Laruelle's role in Yvonne's life and seems quite free of sexual
neuroses. There seems to be no reason, in the light of his
progressive left-wing views, why he should be at all concerned
about Yvonne's indifference to the bourgeois goal of settling
down and raising a family. Lowry seems to have indulged in
ventriloquism at this point in the novel, making Hugh express
an attitude which more properly belongs to the Consul.

The Consul's jealousy of Laruelle colours the entire novel.
The Frenchman's penis ('that hideously elongated cucumiform
bundle of *blue* nerves and gills' (*UTV*, p. 207; p. 210; my
italics)) is symbolically anticipated by his '*blue* polka-dotted
scarf' (*UTV*, p. 15; p. 21; my italics), an 'extraordinary scarf
that suggested M. Laruelle had once won a half-blue' (*UTV*,
p. 210; p. 213). Freud suggested that 'In men's dreams a
necktie often appears as a symbol for the penis [. . .] because
neckties are long, dependent objects and peculiar to men.'[38]

The sexual link between Yvonne and Laruelle is signified by her smart *slate-blue* travelling suit, which the Consul associates with her latest lover, perhaps the mysterious Louis (hence that 'despondent American tune, the St Louis Blues' (*UTV*, p. 11; p. 16)). Hugh has formerly been in a group compared to Venuti's Blue Four and the sexual link between the three men and Yvonne makes them, metaphorically, another 'blue four'. We also learn that Cliff Wright's '*rating as an eligible bachelor was absolutely blue ribbon*' (*UTV*, p. 263; p. 264). But Yvonne's first husband turns out to be unfaithful to her, not 'Mr Right' at all. Significantly the *pelado*, who has 'huge, capable and rapacious' hands (*UTV*, p. 234; p. 237), who is 'gathering strength for more debauchery' (*UTV*, p. 238; p. 241) and who holds himself *erect*, also happens to be wearing a *blue* suit. Finally, at the end of the novel, the Consul takes his revenge on Yvonne with the prostitute, whose room is lit by 'a single blue electric bulb' (*UTV*, p. 348; p. 349).

Under the Volcano is packed with this kind of dream logic, where meaning multiplies in a blur of associations. Colours, numbers, even letters of the alphabet express buried symmetries and hidden meanings which the reader can locate and reassemble according to choice. Critics tend to talk about levels of meaning in *Under the Volcano*, but the metaphor is misleading. The novel's structure is not made up of distinct, discrete elements which can be neatly distinguished like the storeys of a building. There is, rather, an interpenetration and overlapping of the magical and the social-historical, the metafictional and the realistic, the world of the book and the world of the reader. Identity is always in doubt in *Under the Volcano*. The novel is, to use a word which frequently crops up in the narrative, a very *suggestive* book. The Q-ship, for example, is a ship in disguise, its reality the reverse of its appearance, and the dream-logic of Qs continues in the 'real' exterior world of the novel. The identity of Quauhnahuac is imprecise in the sense that the novel supplies the reader with two translations, one positive (to do with an eagle, signifying transcendence), the other negative (to do with the dark wood of error in Dante's *Inferno*). Mr Quincey is the bourgeois comic antithesis of his great romantic addict namesake. Mr Quattras (a *bookmaker*, and hence a kind of mock-Faustian surrogate writer) is a black man who has lost his racial identity through being brought up by whites. Meaning blurs or reverses itself; the narrative aspires to the promise on the coal company advertisement: '*It's a black business but we use you white*' (p. 282; p. 283).

To understand the ways in which Lowry merges naturalism and dream in *Under the Volcano* it is helpful to know something of his composition of the book. The textual history of the novel is complex and our knowledge of its early stages is incomplete, but we know that the dying Indian episode in chapter 8 (originally written as a short story in 1936 and now lost) comprised 'the germ of the book' (*SL*, p. 79). By 1937 this had been substantially expanded to a 40,000-word novel (also lost), and then rewritten again in a 364-page draft. In this earliest-known version the Consul (then named William Ames) is presented unequivocally as the hero. He is saddled with a promiscuous wife, Priscilla, and a promiscuous daughter, Yvonne (both Lowry's angry versions of his first wife, Jan). In this early draft the Consul is above all *innocent*. Yvonne is attracted to a wandering feather-brained student called Hugh Fernhead. The Consul meets his death at the hands of pasteboard fascist villains, the blameless victim of a brutal, treacherous world.

In 1940–1 Lowry produced a new draft, but, though it contains many of the episodes which are to be found in the published text, it was still then a rather flat, histrionic narrative, overburdened with exposition, explication and allusion. This was the version rejected by the major American publishing houses (*SL*, p. 419), and its poor quality can be gauged from the much-anthologized section which Lowry extracted in March 1941 as a short story entitled 'Under the Volcano' and frequently confused with the original lost story.

It was only a relatively late stage in the writing of the novel that Lowry began to cut out the passages of exposition and leaden self-analysis. Omniscience was pared away and the clear outlines of the old narrative began to dissolve. The dense laminated structure of his fictional universe began to be perforated by ambiguity, doubt, baffling breaks in narrative continuity. Lowry's major rewritings of the novel occurred between 1942 and the end of 1944, a poorly documented period in his life. The earliest drafts of the novel must clearly have lacked the dense historical specificity of the final text, since the Second World War had not then broken out. In 1942 Lowry suddenly hit on the idea of intimating that his hero was, possibly, a black magician. He then went on to connect this with his conception of mankind's fate as Faustian. The war vastly underlined the apocalyptic, global implications of the Consul's tragedy, and by alluding to events like the German invasion of the Soviet Union Lowry deepened the prophetic cast of his book. Lowry was continually working-in *objects trouvés*, giving the narrative a curious collage-like texture. The telegram at the start of chapter 4 is a verbatim copy of a real *Daily Herald* cable; the menu in chapter 11 is a genuine one brought back from Mexico and presumably of private, talismanic significance for Lowry. When the Lowry's shack burned down in June 1944 this traumatic event was incorporated into Yvonne's dying vision; homeless, they moved east to stay with Gerald Noxon, a friend from Lowry's Cambridge days. Noxon lived in Oakville, Ontario, and this town was promptly introduced into chapter 10. The novel was finally finished in December 1944, though Lowry continued to make minor revisions as late as the galley proofs stage. (There is a sense in which the rest of Lowry's career was a continual rewriting of *Under the Volcano*.) After several years of intensive revision and refinement the relationship between inner and outer reality in *Under the Volcano* increasingly took on that perplexing, elusive, blurred, palimpsest quality so characteristic of the final text.

In 1937, while staying with Lowry in Mexico, Conrad Aiken began writing a major essay on the fiction of William Faulkner. This essay seems to have exerted a considerable influence over the final stages of Lowry's composition of *Under the Volcano*. Aiken praised Faulkner's 'elaborate method of deliberately witheld meaning':

It is a persistent offering of obstacles, a calculated system of screens and intrusions, of confusions and ambiguous interpolations and delays, with one express purpose; and that purpose is simply to keep the form – and the idea – fluid and unfinished, still in motion as it were, and unknown, until the dropping into place of the very last syllable.[39]

This is just what happens in *Under the Volcano*. The narrative adamantly resists the extraction of a single coherent 'reading' which can account for the book as a totality. Ambiguity is rooted in the very grammar of the narrative. Numerous sentences and paragraphs are snapped off at the ends with a hyphen or a trail of dots, left unfinished, never to be completed. Words like 'seemed', 'obscure', 'perhaps', 'apparently' constantly appear, underlining the baffling nature of relationships, of what connects A to B. Uncertainty, hesitation, ignorance and doubt are the basic conditions of Lowry's fictional universe. The reader is perpetually faced by absolute opacity or, conversely, a baffling plurality of possible meanings. In the words of Gabriel Josipovici (speaking of the fiction of Robbe-Grillet), 'the reader is forced to move again and again over the material that is presented, trying to force it into a single vision, a final truth, but is always foiled by the resistant artefact.'[40] *Under the Volcano* is full of problematic episodes like this:

> Once the swing door opened, someone glanced round quickly to satisfy himself, went out: was that Hugh, Jacques? Whoever it was had seemed to possess the features of both, alternately. Somebody else entered and, though the next instant the Consul felt this was not the case, went right through into the back room, peering round furtively. (*UTV*, p. 228; p. 231)

The technique is reminiscent of Beckett's; authoritative statements are juxtaposed with cancellations of that authority. The two mysterious figures may be real, but equally they may be phantoms of the Consul's mind. Their quick, furtive glances echo Firmin's own guilt-ridden actions. Any sense of an objective reality collapses. The reader's interpretation of this episode will depend on the way he or she chooses to see the Consul – as the cuckolded husband being kept under observation by his wife's lovers, as the anti-fascist being spied upon by his political enemies, or as the hallucinating visionary, projecting his anxieties on to the contingent world. It is the narrative technique Roland Barthes calls '*jamming*, acknowledgement of the insolubility of the enigma',[41] and the metaphor is apt, since reading *Under the Volcano* is rather like listening to a radio programme which is subject to constant distortion and interference.

Under the Volcano is an encyclopedic novel, like the three twentieth-century novels with which it probably has most in common technically – namely *Ulysses*, Nabokov's *Ada* (1969) and Pynchon's *Gravity's Rainbow* (1973). To talk about levels of meaning in *Under the Volcano* is to imply hierarchies of meaning. But encyclopedism is a narrative mode which notoriously resists the privileging of meaning. All perspective tends to get lost, often dissolving into comedy. In the Cyclops section of *Ulysses*, Joyce pokes fun at the Irish heroes and heroines of antiquity by making an inventory of eighty-seven names. The list begins heroically enough ('Cuchulin, Conn of hundred battles, Niall of nine hostages') but soon collapses into absurdity with the introduction of some unexpected and inappropriate names: 'the Last of the Mohicans, the Rose of Castille, the Man for Galway, the Man That Broke the Bank at Monte Carlo, the Man in the Gap, the Woman Who Didn't, Benjamin Franklin, Napoleon Bonaparte'.[42] In a like manner though the Consul may resemble Adam, Christ, Dante, Faustus, Hamlet, Hercules, Prometheus and Odysseus he is also identified with other cultural prototypes which critics usually judiciously ignore – Humpty Dumpty, Peter Rabbit, the Nose with the Luminous Dong. The problem with these analogues is that in total they cancel each other out, and that in isolation they provide only a partial accounting of the novel's dense complexity. The 'meaning' of *Under the Volcano* is no sooner tentatively established than it tends to slip away and reappear in a contradictory form. The novel may be tragic, sombre and mythic, but it is also – *see* Nabokov's remark quoted at the beginning of this chapter – very funny, full of exuberant comedy and parodies. Even at moments of great extremity and suffering the Consul engagingly regards himself as 'an Englishman, and still sporting' (*UTV*, p. 350; p. 351) and an 'old rascal' (p. 351). Although he cries out that he loves hell and can't wait to get back there there is a crucial and rarely quoted qualification: 'the queer thing was, he wasn't quite serious' (p. 314; p. 316).

Under the Volcano presents the reader with a sequence of episodes which do not add up. Lowry's fictional universe is one of shifting, elusive connotations and unbridgeable contradictions between which lie only hiatuses, voids. But, simultaneously, there is a surplus of signifiers which invite the reader to fill in these voids with all-embracing explanations which yoke together disparate and irreconcilable realities, thereby asserting continuity, meaning. The dying Consul imagines he hears Laruelle and Dr Vigil comforting Hugh and Yvonne: '"No se puede vivir sin amar," they would say, which would explain everything' (p. 375). But the whole thrust of the book is to deny answers as simple as this. The teeming contradictions and confusions of life, Lowry seems to suggest, do not permit such easy consolations.

4

METAFICTIONS

These days, often, the novelist resumes the guise of God; but he is merely one of us now, full of confession and error, sin and cleverness. He creates as he is able; insists upon his presence and upon his wickedness and fallibility too. He is not sure about what he knows; his powers have no great extension; he's more imperfect than otherwise; he will appeal to us, even, for sympathy. Why not? He's of his time. Are there any deities left who still have size? (W. H. Gass, *Fiction and the Figures of Life*)

In Donald Barthelme's *Snow White* (1967) a figure named Dan defiantly consumes three bottles of Chablis and promises to 'light that long cigar, that cigar that stretches from Mont St Michel and Chartres to under the volcano.'[43] Barthelme is apparently constructing a fascinating link between Henry Adams, prophet of the modern multiverse (and author of a classic study of medievalism, *Mont-Saint-Michel and Chartres* (1901)) and Lowry's dense, relativistic masterpiece. (Barthelme's smoking metaphor possibly alludes to 'Men With Coats Thrashing', a poem of Lowry's which compares men's lives to cigarettes – used up fast, then thrown away.) It's appropriate to find such a consummate contemporary metafictionalist and encyclopedist as Barthelme jokily signalling his enthusiasm for Lowry, for during the last ten years of his career Lowry's fiction became increasingly reflexive and experimental in tenor.

In December 1945 Lowry returned to Mexico for the first time since his inglorious departure seven years earlier. His experiences there provided him with the 'more-than-Pirandellian theme' (*DAG*, p. 43) of an author in search of his characters. The protagonist in *Dark as the Grave Wherein My Friend is Laid* (1968) is Sigbjørn Wilderness, a writer. This strange, 'unreal' name signals the book's artifice. Sigbjørn is a common (but barely pronounceable) Norwegian name, which might be roughly translated as 'victorious bear'. Lowry explained that he was 'infatuated with the line through the O' (*SL*, p. 327), presumably because of its graphic representation of a split unity. Lowry used the name in a number of other late pieces, though, perplexingly, he explained that Wilderness was 'not the same person' (*SL*, p. 327) each time. The 'bear' concealed in this name probably signifies the destructive forces of the psyche which forever threaten the precarious stability of Lowry's heroes in his late fiction. Wilderness's split-self constantly runs the risk of disintegrating and reverting to its darker side.

In this novel which Lowry wrote as a sequel to *Under the Volcano* Wilderness is Malcolm Lowry himself, in the first and most transparent of the incarnations of this persona. *Dark as the Grave Wherein My Friend is Laid* is unlike anything else Lowry wrote. It is a *roman à clef*, nakedly autobiographical, chatty, anecdotal, picaresque in form. The narrative mostly follows a linear, straightforward chronology, from December 1945 to January 1946. Events and impressions which Lowry/Wilderness experiences are rapidly processed and explicated for the reader. Although set in Mexico *Dark as the Grave* is quite unlike *Under the Volcano*. It is a book of surfaces and transparencies, of exposition and explanation.

The plot is slight. Wilderness and his wife fly down to Mexico City, and then travel on to Cuernavaca and Oaxaca. In this last city Wilderness looks forward to once again seeing his old friend Juan Fernando Martinez (alias J. F. Márquez), but this quest in unsuccessful. Martinez, it turns out, has been dead for over five years.

On the way to Oaxaca Wilderness is also haunted by the memory of two other dead friends, Erikson (the Norwegian writer Nordahl Grieg) and, more obliquely (and never mentioned by name), Paul Fitte. Both were major characters in Lowry's lost novel *In Ballast to the White Sea*. Fitte was a Cambridge friend who committed suicide in 1929, and the novel's title, taken from Abraham Cowley's elegy 'On the Death of Mr William Hervey', makes it clear that Lowry had this old college association in mind:

> Ye fields of Cambridge, our dear Cambridge, say,
> Have ye not seen us walking every day?
> Was there a Tree about which did not know
>   The Love betwixt us two?
> Henceforth, ye gentle Trees, for ever fade;
>   Or your sad branches thicker joyn
>   And into darksome shades combine,
> Dark as the Grave wherein my Friend is Laid.

'Dark' is a key word in the novel. The 'dark dark streets, the melancholy bells' (*DAG*, p. 92) of Mexico City evoke memories of Cambridge, and the Cowley elegy is echoed in the description of the river at Yautepec, 'winding between stiff thick overhanging trees, making pools of shade like on the Cam' (p. 177). Mexico threatens to engulf Wilderness with its 'darkness made for drunkards' (p. 244). The darkness of the grave beckons him to join his dead comrades; the familiar streets and places revive a crowded psychic landscape of ghosts and ancient emotions which Wilderness fitfully seeks to exorcize.

His melancholia is compounded by his sufferings as a writer. Lowry gives us a harrowing inventory of what it was like for him at the end of 1945, with *Under the Volcano* being rejected on all sides as too long, too slow, too wordy. His home has recently been burned to the ground; *In Ballast to the White Sea* has been incinerated; his marriage is on the verge of collapse. He is painfully aware of the success some of his contemporaries are enjoying (Arthur Koestler, for example). Publishers' readers inform him that his book brings to mind *The Lost Weekend* (1944), Charles Jackson's popular novel about dipsomania. Everywhere he goes people seem to be enthusiastically discussing the just-released movie of the Jackson book. Matters are not improved when Jonathan Cape's ambivalent letter about *Under the Volcano* (*SL*, pp. 424–5) arrives. Wilderness/Lowry sets about writing his famous reply, but half way through the letter he attempts suicide. *Dark as the Grave* takes the reader on a nightmarish excursion through the moods of the artist as outcast and failure – maudlin, religious, drunken, syphilophobic, sentimental, neurotic, nostalgic.

If this novel was simply thinly concealed autobiography it would not be without interest, since it catches Lowry at a turning-point in his career and contains much incidental detail about the origins of his masterpiece. But the autobiographical elements unfold within a metafictional frame. Wilderness happens to be contemplating writing a novel to be entitled *Dark as the Grave Wherein My Friend is Laid*. This novel would be 'The real book' (*DAG*, p. 85) – the book which gives the truth about the writer's life and experiences in Mexico, past and present. (The *unreal* book is, of course, *Under the Volcano*: a book which rearranges geography, heightens reality and purges the individual life of its disorder, shaping it into art.) Wilderness laconically suggests that this proposed new novel might be unreadable but it would nevertheless possess the virtue of authenticity.

Dark as the Grave succeeds (setting aside the joke about unreadability) to the extent that Lowry persuades us that this is actually so. As a kind of idiosyncratic literary criticism of *Under the Volcano*, *Dark as the Grave* bears some loose resemblances to Kinbote's deranged, comic engagement with Shade's poem in Nabokov's *Pale Fire* (1962). It presents the reader with lavish amounts of commentary and annotation, and even deconstructs the ending of *Under the Volcano* with the comic suggestion that Yvonne should have gone down the ravine, leaving the Consul to live out his days in boozy cameraderie with Hugh. But as the critical analysis proceeds another story is taking shape – the drama of the making of *Dark as the Grave Wherein My Friend is Laid*. By the end of the book Lowry has demolished his first Mexican novel and built another one out of the pieces.

Dark as the Grave sets out to persuade us that the Mexico of *Under the Volcano* is a romantic fiction. On its first appearance

Popocatapetl is 'considerably diminished [. . .] not much bigger than a slag heap' and the Mexican terrain 'ugly, beyond belief' (*DAG*, p. 70). The epic Mexico of *Under the Volcano* undergoes a drastic re-vision. The landscape seems devoid of all meaning. 'Popo' and 'Ixta' are no longer towering symbols but 'just volcanoes, dead and extinct' (*DAG*, p. 164). If meaning lies anywhere it is not within the landscape but at the surface, on a couple of passing garbage trucks, one called 'Mi Amigo' and the other 'Cruel es mi Destino'. Animals cross the Wildernesses' path – dogs, the pig in the church, two bears in a cage – but unlike the animals in *Under the Volcano* they are merely contingent. The Wildernesses themselves are unheroic characters who converse in banalities. Sigbjørn's final quest, for the sinister Farolito, peters out when he learns that it has moved from its previous site. The real Mexico (as opposed to the Mexico of memory and of his masterpiece) emerges as a flat, depressing place, a realm of abortive quests and petty frustrations.

The form of Wilderness's authentic narrative presents difficulties. He wrestles comically with the requirements of realism, describing how his friend Eddie has 'a head-shaped head [. . .] a body-shaped body [. . .] feet-shaped feet' (*DAG*, p. 152). What Wilderness implicitly seeks is a form analogous to the artefacts which he sees at Monte Albán and Mitla – structures which are stylized, distorted, incomplete. These mysterious and haunting stone memorials to the dead provide an exemplary contrast to the preposterously flashy mausoleum which Wilderness finds in the cemetery. This mausoleum resembles a greenhouse, 'made of millions of tiny mirrors cut in every geometrical shape and fitted together in intricate mosaic patterns. [. . .] The whole great thing glittered and flashed in the sun and looked like some MGM set for the Ziegfeld Follies' (pp. 243–4). The tomb, with its self-reflecting structure, suggests something of the elaborate architectonics of *Under the Volcano*. But the glass-house of art cannot escape from the messiness of life: 'on one side were an empty tequila bottle, old rags, tin cans, even a broken basket –' (p. 244). This brings to mind the bottles, the broken can, the old rags, in Yeats's 'The Circus Animal's Desertion', a poem which likewise explores the tangled relations of life and art, and which asks (as Lowry asks), 'Those masterful images because complete / Grew in pure mind, but out of what began?'

As metafiction *Dark as the Grave Wherein My Friend is Laid* anticipates more the rawer, human-centered experimentalism of British fiction like Doris Lessing's *The Golden Notebook* (1962) and B. S. Johnson's *Trawl* (1966) and *Christie Malry's Own Double Entry* (1972) rather than the cooler, detached, fabulist games-playing strain associated with American writers like Barth, Coover and Barthelme. The British type may seem more innocent than the American variety, less sure of itself, less in control, more strained, but it has strengths which American metafiction sometimes lacks. As Neil Schmitz has argued, 'Unless extended, expressive of a particular vision of experience and illumined by an authorial voice immediately manifest in the style, metafiction becomes nothing but mode: a series of acrobatic exercises in technique.'[44] To my mind Schmitz is right; metafiction does frequently run the risk of becoming wearisome and precious. W. H. Gass (himself an accomplished metafictionalist) has similarly complained that many post-modern writers have been led too far in the direction of what Coleridge called fancy, and he salutes Lowry's writing for being strong where much modern writing is weak: 'it has no fear of feeling.'[45]

Although Lowry had completed a substantial first draft of *Dark as the Grave Wherein My Friend is Laid* by 1947, his nerve broke when it came to submitting it to his publishers. The dominant strain in post-war British writing was quietist. Hugh Hebert has commented that 'the sort of new books that an averagely serious novel reader might be expected to take up in 1948–9 were all overwhelmingly concerned with the middle and professional classes and mostly with what they perceived as their very own crisis.'[46] The leading writers of the day were figures like Nancy Mitford, William Sansom, Elizabeth Bowen, C. P. Snow. The up-and-coming young writer of the period was Angus Wilson, whose first volume of stories *The Wrong Set* was published in 1949. The backward-looking, nostalgic, escapist thrust of books like *Brideshead Revisited* (1945) or *Titus Groan* (1946) was in sharp contrast to Lowry's tough-minded resurrection of the 1930s. After the war few wanted to be reminded of that decade, and Lowry's metaphysical and metafictional concerns pushed him still further outside the bounds of current fashion. If publishers and reviewers had failed to grasp the merits of *Under the Volcano* they were scarcely likely to comprehend a text like *Dark as the Grave Wherein My Friend is Laid*.

As a metafictionalist Lowry felt himself to be a lonely pioneer (as indeed he was: the category had not even been coined then). Disastrously, he lacked a critical language in which to articulate what he was trying to do. In discussing his own and other writers' work he lapsed into 'Cambridge English', speaking in quasi-symbolist terms of 'chords', harmonious organic wholes, integration and resolution. (Lowry explained in 1950 that his intention in *Under the Volcano* was 'to make a noise like music' (*SL*, p. 200); he claimed that the *Hear Us O Lord from Heaven Thy Dwelling Place* volume of stories (written in the early 1950s) 'makes a very beautiful sound' (*SL*, p. 335).) This was a critical vocabulary which had developed out of a response to tightly constructed lyric verse. Its suitability of application to prose was limited, especially for a writer struggling to create 'deliberately rough'[47] fiction of fracture, disintegration, warring moods and tendencies.

The classic statements of the metafictionalist aesthetic occur in André Gide's *Les Faux-monnayeurs* (1926), where Gide's surrogate novelist Edouard proposes writing a novel without a subject:

> I invent the character of a novelist, whom I make my central figure; and the subject of the book, if you must have one, is just that very struggle between what reality offers him and what he himself desires to make of it.[48]

Lowry, however, seems to have had little sense of the alternative anti-realist tradition in the novel which has come down to us from Sterne and with which he might have identified. He found it all too easy to translate the meaning of his fiction into personal terms, even explaining that *Under the Volcano* would appear in his *œuvre* 'less as a novel than as a sort of mighty if preposterous moral deed of some obscure sort, testifying to an underlying toughness of fibre or staying power' (*SL*, p. 332).

In *Dark as the Grave* Lowry put forward the attractive but fatal notion that because life itself is in a constant process of creation, 'An organic work of art, having been conceived, must grow in the creator's mind, or proceed to perish' (*DAG*, p. 168). This idea he applied not only to works-in-progress like *Dark as the Grave*, but also to completed works like *Ultramarine* and *Under the Volcano*. The doctrine is a romantic one, popularized by Coleridge,[49] and there are some classic romantic examples of its practice: Keats began a second version of 'Endymion', Wordsworth rewrote *The Prelude*, Coleridge revised and glossed 'The Ancient Mariner'.

In Lowry's hands the idea proved fatal. If a work of art is in a constant state of growth at what point does the growth stop and the work get finished? This was something Lowry preferred not to think about. Worse still, he applied the logic of organicism to his entire *œuvre*. Before long he had revamped an earlier idea for a Dantesque trilogy (with *Under the Volcano* as the Inferno, *Lunar Caustic* as the Purgatorio, and *In Ballast to the White Sea* as Paradiso) and begun to conceive a massive epic sequence incorporating everything which he had written. This epic, to be entitled *The Voyage That Never Ends*, was to be subject to perpetual adjustment as each new fiction glossed what had gone before. (A key document here is Lowry's unpublished fifty-page *Work in Progress* statement, written in 1951, much of which is devoted to a discussion of unwritten and probably unwritable fiction.[50])

Lowry's ambitious plan for an interrelated sequence of novels was not in itself unrealistic. Joyce, Beckett and Nabokov provide perfect examples of writers whose individual *œuvres* make up a reflexive whole. Robert Giroux of Harcourt Brace wrote that *The Voyage That Never Ends* 'promises what might be the most important literary project of the decade' (*SL*, p. 445) and had Lowry completed it Giroux might well have been proved right. But Lowry quickly found himself bogged down in more and more unfinished manuscripts, psychologically unable to finish anything. Like William Paterson in

'Through the Panama' he had 'too many novel ideas' (*HUOL*, p. 56).

Before he had finished the first draft of *Dark as the Grave Wherein My Friend is Laid* he had started on a story which he was to expand into his only other full-length novel, *October Ferry to Gabriola*. But before either of these manuscripts was brought to a satisfactory conclusion he made a fourteen-month trip to Europe, which in turn inspired the stories in *Hear Us O Lord from Heaven Thy Dwelling Place*. He had barely begun work on these stories before he was sidetracked into drafting 'The Ordeal of Sigbjørn Wilderness'. Lowry found himself in Tristram Shandy's predicament: the onward surge of life continually outran his ability to get it all down on paper.

For much of the last ten years of his life Lowry's career was in crisis. He piled up one incomplete, abortive manuscript after another. *Dark as the Grave* went through two more drafts but Lowry was reluctant to consider it finished. A third Mexican novel, *La Mordida*, was attempted, covering Lowry's traumatic experiences in Mexico after January 1946, but the narrative fell apart and remains unpublished, a mass of notes and jottings. 'The Ordeal of Sigbjørn Wilderness' proved to be a similar failure. It exists in the form of notes for a short novel about a writer's crack-up and has not been published. The theory of the organic work of art provided an ideal excuse for putting off the day when his highly experimental narratives would have to face the criticism of publishers' readers.

The major disappointment of Lowry's final years is *October Ferry to Gabriola* (largely written 1952–4), his last novel, to which he devoted much time and energy. It gives an account of a long day's journey to Gabriola Island, British Columbia, made by Ethan Llewelyn, a lawyer. During the course of the day Llewelyn reviews his troubled life and reaches out towards the hope of a new future with his wife. Unfortunately the novel lacks any real narrative drive, the characterization is weak and the time-scheme muddled. Lowry's own distinction between 'a successful book' and one which merely indicates that 'your author is a genius' (*SL*, p. 316) seems all too apposite where *October Ferry* is concerned. There are some powerful passages but in the end the novel fails to cohere.

Lowry temporarily solved his writing crisis by abandoning the genre of fiction altogether and writing a screenplay of Scott Fitzgerald's *Tender is the Night*. Although he was a keen movie-goer, Lowry knew nothing about screenplays, failing to appreciate the considerable extent to which film-making is a collaborative and sometimes improvisational activity. His script, consequently, is overburdened with extensive and redundant directions regarding camera angles and numerous other aspects of production which lie outside the scriptwriter's remit. The 455-page typescript is nevertheless an impressive text, a kind of hybrid metafiction which deconstructs the Fitzgerald novel and remakes it in the image of one by Malcolm Lowry. Christopher Isherwood hailed it as 'a masterpiece', shrewdly identifying it as 'mental theatre' (*SL*, p. 443), comparable to Thomas Hardy's *The Dynasts*. When it is eventually published it will clearly be something of a literary occasion, and can only boost Lowry's reputation.

The *Tender is the Night* screenplay illuminates the extent to which Lowry's crisis was an aesthetic one. His writing block and corrosive lack of self-confidence applied only to his writing of fiction, not writing *per se*. The screenplay (which Lowry claimed was written in just seven months) demonstrates that he had no difficulty with words. Nor (as some critics have suggested) did Lowry write-off the novel as a worthwhile literary form. As he remarked of Ralph Ellison's *Invisible Man* (1952), 'in what other form than the novel could so many hard and – for the world – necessary points be made so tellingly?' (*SL*, p. 316).

The question of how he related to 'the world' in his writing lies at the heart of Lowry's writing difficulties during these last ten years of his life. The life-style and tourism of a middle-aged English expatriate was, as Lowry was painfully, acutely aware, insufficient as an artistic resource. His crisis cannot be seen in isolation from wider cultural developments. In 1952 *Partisan Review* published a symposium on 'Our Country and Our Culture' which stated that many intellectuals no longer accepted alienation as the true condition of the artist. They had 'ceased to think of themselves as rebels and exiles' and they wanted 'very much to be part of American life'.[51] A story like

'Strange Comfort Afforded by the Profession' cries out to be read as a response to such cultural pressures. Unable to discover any shared identity among his contemporaries Wilderness is forced to find communion with the dead writers.

In the 1930s things had been easier for Lowry. In *Lunar Caustic* and *Under the Volcano* he had convincingly linked the solipsism and doom of his alienated heroes with the fate of the world at large. The looming shadow of world war gave the disintegration of Bill Plantagenet and Geoffrey Firmin a public meaning and significance. But now the apocalypse was over, 'the most dramatic events of history having swept by him like a liner in the fog' (*DAG*, p. 42). War had been replaced by cold war. *Dark as the Grave Wherein My Friend is Laid* registers the new political climate ('$15 Billion for Red Arms, Exceeds US' (*DAG*, p. 53); 'butterflies people being tortured in China: butterflies atom bomb' (*DAG*, p. 174)) but only in inconsequential and peripheral ways.

Revealingly, the one dimension which *Dark as the Grave* does not seek to return to and interrogate is that of politics. What is striking about the novel is just how out of touch with the contemporary condition of Mexico Lowry actually was during his return in 1944–5. Wilderness gazes out of a bus window in Oaxaca and draws impressionistic conclusions: 'it seemed to him there was a vast improvement in the human lot, and all this he put down to [the] Ejidal' (*DAG*, pp. 207–8). At the end of the book Lowry tacked on a belated salute to the achievements of the Mexican Revolution:

> It was all so different from eight years ago, and also the look of the animals, which were not shabby or starved looking but had strong well-fed looks and shining coats that came from proper feeding and care, and the fields themselves were rich. (p. 255)

This is propaganda, expressed in slack, unfeeling language. What is extraordinarily ironic is just how inaccurate Lowry's celebratory climax actually is, historically. After 1938, the year Lowry left Mexico, the socialist advance began to falter. In December 1940 President Camacho was inaugurated and promptly announced that the Revolution was over. Camacho began a major dismantling of the progressive social programmes initiated by Cárdenas. Land redistribution slowed dramatically; the communal *ejidos* lost government backing; the radical trade union organization Conferación de Trabajadores de México was neutered, the right to strike curtailed. Populist socialism gave way to the requirements of industrial capitalism.

This is scarcely the impression conveyed by *Dark as the Grave*, from which one might assume that the radical policies of Cárdenas were still in full bloom. Ironically, Lowry was actually in Mexico in January 1946, at the very moment when this change in outlook was institutionalized by the official Party of the Revolution's selection of Miguel Alemán as the next candidate for the presidency. Under Alemán the old agrarian reforms slid further into decay. Lowry seems not to have noticed any of this.

Lowry's disengagement from his erstwhile radicalism was underlined by his suggestion that Juan Cerillo be cut from chapter 4 for a projected abridged Signet paperback edition of *Under the Volcano* (*SL*, p. 173). A year later, in 1950, he wrote a disingenous portrait of Juan Fernando Márquez for a United Nations magazine. In it Lowry omitted all mention of Márquez's radical politics and passed off the Ejidal scheme, innocuously, as being 'based on an old Aztec system'.[52] Lowry's mental fatigue is all too evident in the extraordinary gush of clichés with which he describes Mexico: 'magic [. . .] the days go by in a timeless haze, its romance and mystery are not overstated [. . .] colourful and proud.'[53] These are assuredly not the phrases which spring to Sigbjørn Wilderness's lips as he grumpily treks around that country, harassed, cheated and overcharged wherever he goes.

*

Lowry's retreat from history and society resulted in an undeniable shrinkage of perspective in his writing. After *Under the Volcano* he made no further experiments with point of view. His characters become ciphers; the loss of Mexico as an inspiration was paralleled by the disappearance of sexuality as a major fictional theme. Lowry's later fiction is all narrated from the narrow perspective of a solitary male consciousness. This sometimes resulted in a kind of tunnel vision, especially where the portrayal of women was concerned (someone once observed that Lowry's ideal woman seemed to be a mattress which cooked).

It is all the more remarkable then that after he had completed the Fitzgerald screenplay Lowry's fiction-writing career suddenly blossomed again. Between 1949 and 1953 he overcame his writing block and embarked on a sequence of stories and novellas, exploring personal themes, often within an experimentalist, metafictional framework. In Ortega y Gasset's *Toward a Philosophy of History* Lowry stumbled upon the proposition that every life is 'a work of fiction' and man 'a sort of novelist of himself' (*SL*, p. 210). Ortega's idea delighted Lowry, enabling him to convince himself that his autobiographically based metafictions had a public significance.

The keynote of Lowry's new short fiction was a kind of precarious optimism. The hymn which gives the *Hear Us O Lord from Heaven Thy Dwelling Place* volume its title poses an appeal for help in the face of raging seas and furious storms. Whether or not the appeal will ever be answered remains ambiguous. Storms, raging seas and even volcanoes keep reappearing in this collection of stories and a course is successfully navigated past them. The stories are comic in thrust and end in affirmation. But as Brian Moore has pointed out they also sound a deeper, darker note:

> Though the note of affirmation in the joy of life sounds again and again in these writings, we are reminded of the desperate cheerfulness of a man who is recovering from a frightening depression. Wives must always be gay and good; nature must always be lovely and life-enhancing for behind every moment of this self-forgetting lurks the iron shadow of the albatross.[54]

'The Forest Path to the Spring' is one of the most popular and successful of Lowry's late stories, and has been influential in establishing the Lowry myth. It gives a romantic version of life in the squatter's settlement at Dollarton ('where but to think was to be full of Thoreau', as Lowry elsewhere acidly noted).[55]

The narrative tone is one of quiet, retrospective repose – the archetypal Lowry protagonist at last in paradise – and much of the story's appeal lies in Lowry's delicate descriptions of the Canadian landscape. The narrative is free of the symbolizing impulse that chokes *October Ferry to Gabriola*, and literary allusions are pared to a minimum. The long, flowing sentences convey the changing seasons and the rhythms of the natural landscape with a brilliance that brings to mind the writing of Hardy and Lawrence.

The story is not however directly autobiographical. Time and place are not identified, and the anonymous first-person narrator presents himself as a musician. A preoccupation with writing nevertheless emerges. The narrator describes his struggles to write a symphony, his composition of an opera called 'The Forest Path to the Spring' and musical projects which, 'destined to develop in terms of ever more complex invention' (*HUOL*, p. 266), echo the equally ambitious scenarios of Lowry's abortive epic *The Voyage That Never Ends*.

Writing appears more centrally in 'Elephant and Colosseum', which takes up and interrogates some of the themes of *Dark as the Grave Wherein My Friend is Laid*. It tells of a novelist in Rome encountering a comic difference between the plots of fiction and those of life. Cosnahan has been reading *Tender is the Night* and wonders if, like Dick Diver, he will have a chance meeting with someone from his past. Eventually, in a strange way, he does. But whereas Diver has a romantic encounter with the beautiful young actress, Rosemary, Cosnahan meets up with an elephant. Ironically, the elephant, met years previously on a sea-voyage, is also called Rosemary. She has, we learn, recently appeared as a 'character' of sorts in Cosnahan's recently published novel *Ark from Singapore*, albeit misrepresented 'for the sake of unity' (*HUOL*, p. 166). The comic reappearance of the elephant in Cosnahan's life serves to remind him of how much more complex reality is than its fictional representations.

Just as *Dark as the Grave* represents itself as the authentic book of Lowry's Mexican experiences, so Lowry seeks to persuade the reader that the immensely complex and circuitous narrative of 'Elephant and Colosseum' provides the true version of Cosnahan's experiences, unlike his novel. The preposterous inadequacy of conventional realism is further underlined by Cosnahan's recollection of 'The Dinghy', a story written by a colleague and based on a true incident at sea:

> he felt that what he had written *was* the truth, that it *would* sell, but only to a 'high class' audience. [. . .] So for the sake of this art, this truth, he introduced pirates, opium runners, a beachcomber in decaying white flannels, while the poor old mother aged seventy, whom he himself had rescued, became a pretty American, fleeing from her brutal father, at the connivance of a tall, dark, and slim Frenchman, who had no part in the dashing proceedings, with a fortune in Shanghai. (*HUOL*, pp. 145–6)

Here Lowry satirizes both popular fiction of the *Thorn Birds/Far Pavilions* variety and, in a more subtle sense, the romantic elements in *Under the Volcano*. Significantly, the author of 'The Dinghy' is a writer who is as much in love with the public posture of being a writer as with writing itself: 'that nobody should make any mistake about his vocation [he] worked standing up with the door to his room wide open, his papers spread out on the vacant upper bunk, and his hair falling wildly over his face in a tangle of inspiration' (*HUOL*, p. 145). Lowry, we know, always wrote standing up. The comic truth underlying the exaggerations of 'The Dinghy' is that the pretty American is actually based on an enormously fat old woman weighing 250 lbs.

A more experimental assault on the bad faith of naturalism occurs in 'Ghostkeeper'. This describes the efforts of a journalist named Goodheart to write a story called 'Lex Talionis'. As he contemplates the materials of his narrative Goodheart becomes increasingly aware both of the perplexingly ambiguous, shifting nature of reality and of the inadequacy of the conventional short-story form as a medium for expressing this new-found awareness. His conscience tells him that 'if you're going to get anywhere near the truth you'll have twenty different plots and a story no-one will take' (*PAS*, p. 219). The story ends with Goodheart settling for 'the shorter version. [. . .] Everything was selection, concision, the story writer's touch

[. . .] a touching little conte' (*PAS*, p. 226). Goodheart's name, we realize, is wholly ironic. (Alert readers will realize from the fact that Goodheart sips at a glass of *milk* while writing his story that Lowry does not intend him to be an exemplary figure.) The journalist stands convicted of bad faith, having given way to the pressures of success, fashion and convention.

'Ghostkeeper' is itself the story with 'twenty different plots' which Goodheart should have written, but didn't. Hence the narrative instability, the choice of alternate titles and plots, use of notes, memoranda, and reflexive commentaries. The story begins with a question about time and proceeds to describe Goodheart and his wife walking *clock-wise* round Stanley Park in Vancouver. A sign at Prospect Point lists statistics about local geography, but the landscape itself denies the veracity of fixed temporal or geographical identity. Everything in 'Ghostkeeper' is in a state of flux and metamorphosis: winter is turning into spring, the snow is melting, the light is fading, a familiar house has become a hotel, an 'antediluvian' monkey tree continues 'its liason with the prehistoric era' (*PAS*, p. 217). With a nod to Gogol Lowry at one point even makes Goodheart lose his physical identity and turn into his overcoat.

The shifts and elisions of the narrative mimic this ever-changing reality. 'Ghostkeeper' marks the logical conclusion of Lowry's belief in the organic work of art: it is a narrative which is all process. Or, more accurately, it is a carefully constructed narrative which gives the impression of improvisation.[56] 'Ghostkeeper' was the last story Lowry wrote and marked the limit of his formal experiments. He was unwilling completely to abandon either naturalism or the phenomenal world (as, say, Beckett was, after *Malone Dies* (1956)). Thereafter Lowry turned all his attention to *October Ferry to Gabriola* and returned to a more conventional mode, with disappointing results.

It is probably significant that the best of Lowry's late work consists of short fiction. Robert Scholes has asserted that 'When extended, metafiction must either lapse into a more fundamental mode of fiction or risk losing all fictional interest in order to maintain its intellectual perspectives.'[57] The failure of *October Ferry to Gabriola* underlines Scholes's argument.

The description of the movie, 'with its menacing, almost inaudible characters and clanking machinery of which you knew half the plot [...] too theatrical, too slow, poorly directed, lighted, portentously acted' (OF, pp. 132–4) is obviously intended as a droll commentary on the novel itself, but this kind of self-parodying acknowledgement of narrative inadequacies does not redeem the defects of the book. In the end *October Ferry to Gabriola* is an ill-digested *mélange* of styles and autobiographical titbits.[58]

In 'Through the Panama', probably the finest piece of writing Lowry produced in the 1950s, he extended his assault on realism, and met some pressing problems – History, the New Criticism – head-on. The late 1940s and early 1950s were the golden years of New Criticism. New Critics insisted that literary works were autonomous, and that the intentions or biography of a writer were quite irrelevant to the finished product. The cultural hegemony of this movement was bad news for someone like Lowry. Hence his rage in 'Through the Panama' against 'the non-creative bully-boys and homosapient schoolmasters of English literature' and a 'dictatorship of opinion, an opinion that is not based on shared personal or felt experience or identity with a given writer, or love of literature, or even any intrinsic knowledge of *writing*' (HUOL, p. 75). 'In fact' (he adds) 'I have to forget that there is such a thing as so-called "modern literature" and the "new criticism" in order to get any of my old feeling and passion back' (HUOL, p. 75).

'Through the Panama' gives Lowry's passionate response to these forces which he saw pressing down on him, frustrating his career. The novella is subtitled 'From the Journal of Sigbjørn Wilderness' and gives an account of a sea-voyage down the west coast of the United States, along the Panama Canal and across the Atlantic to Europe. The naturalistic opening paragraphs set the scene, establish a precise chronology and introduce the familiar figures of the writer Sigbjørn Wilderness and his wife. But soon this linear, developing, realistic narrative begins to disintegrate. Sigbjørn's identity starts to dissolve. He alludes, obscurely, to events like the suicide of Paul Fitte on 15 November 1929, which have an existence only in the private life of the author, Malcolm Lowry.

His identity soon undergoes a further transformation and he turns into Martin Trumbaugh, a character in a book he is writing. Before long the story has decomposed still further. The narrative tense becomes unstable, jumping to and fro from the present to the past, and the story line begins to disappear as the description of the voyage is interrupted by scraps of verse, newspaper cuttings, definitions of cultural identity, bits of literary criticism, notes on Wilderness's work-in-progress and incongruous commentaries on a host of topics from murders in Mexico to brands of Californian whisky. After twenty-five disordered pages the narrative then splits vertically into two, and the reader is faced by a dozen pages of parallel narrative.

In short, 'Through the Panama' is a New Critic's nightmare. Outside the context of Lowry's life and *œuvre* it is incomprehensible. The natural impulse of the reader is to try and establish some principle of coherence within all the apparent confusion of the text. The narrative seems willing to collaborate in this, providing helpful comments about the characters, and using Coleridge's gloss from 'The Ancient Mariner' to suggest a movement from psychic crisis to equilibrium. In the end, though, the encyclopedism of 'Through the Panama' refuses to privilege any one reading of the text. Any account of the story is bound to seem partial.

Lowry's title echoes Lewis Carroll's *Through the Looking-Glass* (1871) and provides a key to his intentions. In his later stories Lowry's writer-heroes are often to be found peering into mirrors and puzzling over their problematic identities. The first story in *Hear Us O Lord from Heaven Thy Dwelling Place* begins with 'the mirror [. . .] of an old weighing machine' (*HUOL*, p. 14), a device capable of reflecting an extraordinarily unreal, wide-angled perspective (weighing up the past, perhaps). 'Through the Panama' takes us into Lowry's own private wonderland of dreams and nightmares. The metamorphoses of Sigbjørn Wilderness bear an ironic resemblance to those of Alice herself. In normal life Alice often pretends to be two people. After drinking from a bottle she undergoes a series of surrealistic changes, holds monologues with herself, and worries about her identity: 'Who in the world am I? Ah, *that's* the great puzzle!'[59] The demonic 'seemingly bodiless creature a bit like the Cheshire Cat' (*HUOL*, p. 83) that Martin Trumbaugh dreams of seeing in a painting by Bosch is obviously in one sense Cheshire-born Lowry himself. Lowry once wrote admiringly of a book without 'a hero in the usual sense' who 'isn't even physically described [. . .] so that he has no features or stature and is quite impossible to picture save as several kinds of person at once; on another plane [. . .] more like a voice' (*SL*, p. 256) and 'Through the Panama' best expresses his implicit desire to create just such a figure.

Of all Lowry's late stories 'Through the Panama' is the one which most radically ruptures the conventions of realism. By actually fragmenting the story on the printed page, making the reader face two parallel narratives, Lowry demolished the principle of linear progression (the very essence of *the book*) in a striking and original fashion. Lowry's rebellion against the formal limitations of printed narrative anticipates the experimentalism of that equally tormented writer B. S. Johnson (*Albert Angelo* (1964), *The Unfortunates* (1969)) a decade or more later.

Significantly, the secondary parallel narrative in small print is about history. Quoting liberally from Helen Nicolay's *The Bridge of Water* (1940), Lowry uses the history of the Panama Canal as a microcosm of the development of European society. To the historian Europe's capitalist and imperialist drive brought order and civilization to the New World. But Lowry proceeds to deconstruct the rationalist progressive models of historians, concentrating instead on the terrible human cost involved in the making of the canal. Elsewhere, in a draft of one of the other stories in *Hear Us O Lord*, Lowry attacked the historian Arnold Toynbee:

> Who had the more common sense then, a man like Toynbee or Wilderness? It argued a remarkable degree of vanity to be a historian, a remarkable degree of blindness, in a limited sense, to attempt to say anything new about it, for there was terribly little that was new to say.[60]

The real truth of history, Lowry suggests (echoing the Consul's sour view) is human suffering – a thesis which enables him to connect his writer-hero to the world at large. The 'Hear Us O

Lord' hymn which gives these stories their collective title is, evocatively, from the Isle of *Man*. The alienation and pain of Lowry's heroes link them to mankind and make them truly representative.

The experimentalist features of 'Through the Panama' triumphantly and persuasively affirm the tangled comic-grotesque truths of a novelist's experience and imagination against the mundane rational models of order created by historians, realist novels and 1950s literary criticism. Or as that 'bit of Ariel's song' (*HUOL*, p. 102) from *The Tempest* has it, 'Nothing of him that doth fade, / But doth suffer a sea-change / Into something rich and strange'. This is perhaps as good a way as any of describing the transformations Lowry's persona undergoes in the best of his late fiction. After *Under the Volcano* his career changed course. He learned how to begin again, refashioning the image of his masterpiece and negotiating a route beyond it through a largely hostile critical climate. These late writings demonstrate the seriousness of Lowry's ambitions. The metamorphoses of a fictional self who is often a writer provide a complex accounting of Lowry's restless engagement with the vexed question of private and public meaning in post-modern fiction. In the early 1950s Lowry wrote that where autobiographically based fiction was concerned, much 'would seem to depend upon the technique – moreover what if one should give a real turn of the screw to a subject that is so often treated half-heartedly? I think unquestionably what one is after is a new form, a new approach to reality itself' (*SL*, pp. 330–1). That ambition was, in the end, substantially achieved. Lowry's reflexive sequence of novels and stories, variations around the theme of spiritual voyage, is unique in modern writing.

APPENDIX: THE FILM OF 'UNDER THE VOLCANO'

The idea of filming *Under the Volcano* was first mooted in the early 1950s. Since then the complicated history of the numerous abortive film projects has become almost as legendary as Malcolm Lowry's own tangled life and career. In 1983 a production by Moritz Borman and Wieland Schulz-Keil succeeded where all the others had failed, and *Under the Volcano* was at last filmed, on location in and around Cuernavaca, Mexico. John Huston directed.

Under the Volcano has often been described as a 'cinematic' novel, in part because of its reliance on flash-backs and visual devices like the garden sign which reappears by itself on the last page of the book. But having ploughed through over sixty screenplays Schulz-Keil wearily complained that too many screenwriters regarded *Under the Volcano* as being already essentially a screenplay requiring little more than the addition of scene numbers and camera angles. Huston's production team decided against making an art movie and aimed instead for a sparer, more accessible version of Lowry's masterpiece. Lowry himself would probably not have objected in principle to the narrative compression such an approach necessarily involved, since he remarked of his own *Tender is the Night* screenplay that he had 'left enough out for an opera by Pucini' (*SL*, p. 204).

In his minimalist approach to the novel Huston sought to concentrate solely on the Consul's doomed, downward slide and to do without framing devices, sub-plots or flash-backs which would (as he saw it) have detracted from this direct, linear movement of fate. Huston explained that his intention in the film was 'to penetrate through those mists and miasmas (in the novel) and to simplify it, get it down to its essentials'.[61]

The resulting film version differs in a variety of ways from the book. By, in effect, disposing of the role played by the past in the novel Huston's film omits large tracts of Lowry's narrative. Laruelle is gone and in consequence so is much of the material from chapters 1 and 7. Hugh's memories in chapter 6 and Yvonne's in chapter 9 are likewise not conveyed. In place of chapter 1 the film substitutes a short sequence of scenes which are intended to establish the Mexican locale and historical setting, and to introduce the Consul. These opening scenes are set on the evening of 1 November 1938, and thus the film adopts a twenty-four hour framework for its dramatic action. We first encounter Geoffrey Firmin walking through a cemetery and on into the streets of Cuernavaca. He talks to a pariah dog, passes a cinema where *Las Manos de Orlac* is in progress, enters Bustamente's cantina and falls into conversation with Dr Vigil. The two men move on to the Red Cross ball, where the Consul makes a spectacle of himself by verbally abusing the German ambassador. Finally Vigil leads the Consul out of the ballroom and into a nearby chapel, where he encourages Firmin to pray to the Virgin for Yvonne's return.

This opening section is the only substantially re-invented part of the story. The rest of Huston's film follows the major configurations of Lowry's narrative, though some scenes have been transposed (the bedroom scene, the Englishman in the MG) and others have been telescoped (the Salón Ofélia is located at the Arena Tomalín). The episode in which Hugh and Yvonne go horseriding has gone, as have many of the minor characters such as Weber, the dwarf postman, the young man with dark glasses and the giant with the peanut wagon. There are numerous minor differences between the film and the book. Yvonne, an American, is played by the English actress Jacqueline Bisset. The title 'Chief of Rostrums' is altered to 'Chief of Stockyards'. Yvonne and Hugh arrive at the Farolito while the Consul is in Maria's room.

The three principals in Huston's film are well cast. Albert Finney persuasively evokes the twitches and jitters of an alcoholic in the throes of collapse. Hugh and Yvonne are pale versions of their novelistic selves but Anthony Andrews is convincing as a slightly bemused dilettante and Jacqueline Bisset makes a suitably elegant, suffering Yvonne. One problem with Huston's approach, though, is that once the inner lives and pasts of the major characters are by-passed questions of motivation arise which are absent in the novel. In disposing of the Consul's past Huston gives us a character whose tragic condition is given rather than established and developed in the course of the film. The Consul's suffering, visionary insights and wit dominate the novel, making him at once both engagingly sympathetic and intensely tragic. In the film version Huston, by eschewing flash-backs or hallucination sequences, has the problem of conveying this cauldron of concealed emotions, desires and memories from the outside. Though Finney's performance is a *tour de force* he does not succeed in making the Consul appear either a very sympathetic or interesting figure.

Lowry's dense, complex text presents an enormous challenge to both screenwriter and director, and Huston's stripped-down version of *Under the Volcano* is barely convincing, even on its own terms. The pariah dog, far from being a hideous mangy outcast, appears incongruously well-groomed. The period atmosphere is purely cosmetic. The film altogether lacks the mythic and symbolic intensity of the novel (the Máquina Infernal episode, for example, is superficial and redundant, just another drunken Consular spree). The scene with Mr Quincey is perfunctory. Yvonne's death is melodramatic and unconvincing. The ending is badly handled and lacks either a ravine or a dead dog. After the row at the restaurant the Consul runs not towards a darkening forest but is seen clambering aboard a conveniently passing bus. The political motive for the Indian rider's murder is missing, making the incident meaningless. And, perhaps most astonishingly of all, there is no sight of an abyss anywhere in the film.

In giving us a linear, surface, exterior account of the Consul's tragedy Huston flattens out the metaphysical and political ambiguities of Lowry's narrative. What we get, in effect, is a realist film of an expressionist novel. As an adaptation of a classic text Huston's *Under the Volcano* is not as disappointing as his 1956 film of *Moby-Dick* (widely criticised for turning Melville's masterpiece into a superficial adventure story). Finney's performance is a powerful one, and the evocation of the theatricality and colour of a Mexican Day of the Dead is vivid and entertaining. The dramatization of key scenes from the novel may be helpful to first-time readers grappling with Lowry's opaque and enigmatic narrative. That said, *Under the Volcano* is unlikely to be rated as one of the finer achievements of Huston's long and varied career.[62]

NOTES

1 Malcolm Bradbury, *Possibilities: Essays on the State of the Novel* (London, 1973), p. 182.
2 Joseph Killorin (ed.), *Selected Letters of Conrad Aiken* (New Haven, Conn., 1978), p. 243.
3 Ibid., p. 239.
4 Ibid., p. 244.
5 Ibid., p. 218.
6 Ibid., p. 239.
7 *The Times Literary Supplement*, 16 February 1967, p. 127.
8 All bracketed ellipses are mine.
9 Samuel Hynes, *The Auden Generation* (London, 1976), p. 187.
10 In 1952 Lowry wrote, 'Of *Lunar Caustic*, I possess two versions, neither of them final' (*SL*, p. 286). He did not live to rewrite the novella, as he had hoped to. The currently available text is an abridgement by Margerie Lowry and Earle Birney of the two drafts referred to by Lowry: 'The Last Address', a ninety-four-page typescript (written *c*.1935–9), about Sigbjørn Lawhill and his 'hysterical identification with Melville' (*SL*, pp. 24–5), and 'Swinging the Maelstrom', a seventy-page typescript (written *c*.1940–1), in which the hero's name is changed to Bill Plantagenet. The major difference between the two drafts is one of tone rather than of style or incident; 'The Last Address' is a bleaker, more despairing text.
11 University of British Columbia Lowry Collection (hereafter UBC), Box 36(5).
12 Andrew J. Pottinger, 'The Consul's "Murder"', *Canadian Literature*, 67 (Winter 1976), p. 60.
13 Unpublished letter to John Davenport, 31 August 1937. UBC Box 3.
14 Jorge Luis Borges, *Labyrinths* (Harmondsworth, 1970), p. 229.

15 Sherill Grace, *The Voyage That Never Ends* (Vancouver, 1982), p. 41.

16 Douglas Day, *Malcolm Lowry* (New York, 1973), p. 350.

17 Roger Bromley, 'The Boundaries of Commitment: God, Lover, Comrade – Malcolm Lowry's *Under the Volcano* as a Reading of the 1930s', in Francis Barker (ed.), *1936: The Sociology of Literature*, Vol. 1 (Colchester, 1979), p. 273.

18 Roland Barthes, *S/Z*, trans. Richard Miller (London, 1975), p. 4.

19 Kristofer Dorosz, *Malcolm Lowry's Infernal Paradise* (Uppsala, 1976), p. 10.

20 'Preface to a Novel', in Woodcock (ed.), *Malcolm Lowry: The Man and his Work* (Vancouver, 1971), p. 13.

21 For an exhaustive discussion of this aspect of the novel see D. J. Hadfield, 'Bridging the Abyss: Polarities and Parallels in Malcolm Lowry's *Under the Volcano*' (Unpublished MA dissertation, University of East Anglia, 1978). My own understanding of the novel has also been greatly assisted by Duncan Hadfield's thesis, 'Real and Imaginary Golf Courses: Systems of Order in Malcolm Lowry's *Under the Volcano*' (Unpublished doctoral dissertation, University of Warwick, 1982).

22 Jean-Paul Sartre, *What is Literature?*, trans. Bernard Frechtman (London, 1967), pp. 165–6.

23 W. B. Yeats, *A Vision* (New York, 1966), p. 268.

24 Sartre, op. cit., p. 229.

25 Virginia Woolf, *Mrs Dalloway* (Harmondsworth, 1964), p. 196.

26 George Orwell, *Homage to Catalonia* (London, 1959), p. 248.

27 Bromley, op. cit., p. 287.

28 Graham Greene, *The Lawless Roads* (London, 1955), p. 32.

29 Robert Heilman, 'Four Novels', *Sewanee Review*, 55, 3 (Summer 1947), p. 491.

30 Stephen Tifft, 'Tragedy as a Meditation on Itself: Reflexiveness in *Under the Volcano*', in Anne Smith (ed.), *The Art of Malcolm Lowry* (London, 1978), p. 68.

31 Roger Bromley, 'Malcolm Lowry', *The Times Higher Education Supplement*, 9 December 1983.

32 Tariq Ali, review of *Midnight's Children*, *New Left Review*, 136 (November–December 1982), pp. 87–95.

33 Salman Rushdie, 'Imaginary Homelands', *London Review of Books*, 7–20 October 1982; quoted in ibid., p. 93.

34 James Joyce, *Ulysses* (Harmondsworth, 1969), p. 278.

35 Richard Ellman, *James Joyce* (London, 1966), p. 405.

36 T. Bareham, 'Paradigms of Hell: Symbolic Patterning in *Under the Volcano*', in B. S. Benedikz (ed.), *On the Novel* (London, 1971), p. 115.

37 Vladimir Nabokov, *Transparent Things* (Harmondsworth, 1975), p. 21.

38 Sigmund Freud, *The Interpretation of Dreams*, trans. James Strachey (New York, 1965), p. 391.

39 Conrad Aiken, 'William Faulkner: The Novel as Form', *Atlantic Magazine* (November 1939), p. 652.

40 Gabriel Josipovici, ' "But time will not relent": modern literature and the experience of time', in Josipovici (ed.), *The Modern English Novel* (London, 1976), p. 264.

41 Roland Barthes, op. cit., p. 210.

42 James Joyce, op. cit., p. 295.

43 Donald Barthelme, *Snow White* (New York, 1967), p. 137.

44 Neil Schmitz, 'Robert Coover and the Hazards of Metafiction', *Novel*, 37 (Spring 1974), p. 213.

45 W. H. Gass, *Fiction and the Figures of Life* (New York, 1970), p. 73.

46 Hugh Hebert, '1948 and all that', *The Guardian*, 31 December 1983, p. 7.

47 Malcolm Lowry, 'Note on "Through the Panama"', UBC Box 36(7).

48 André Gide, *The Counterfeiters*, trans. Dorothy Bussy (Harmondsworth, 1966), pp. 168–9.

49 A full genealogy is given in G. S. Rousseau (ed.), *Organic Form: The Life of an Idea* (London, 1972).

50 See UBC Box 36. A full account of the relationship between Lowry's epic plan and his fiction is given in Sherrill Grace, *The Voyage That Never Ends* (Vancouver, 1982).

51 Quoted in Peter Fuller, *Beyond the Crisis in Art* (London, 1980), pp. 81–2.

52 Malcolm Lowry, 'Garden of Etla', *United Nations World*, 4 (June 1950), pp. 45–7.

53 Ibid.

54 Brian Moore, 'The Albatross of Self', *Spectator*, 4 May 1962, p. 589.

55 See the MSS of *October Ferry to Gabriola*, UBC Box 16(10).

56 The story was at a more advanced stage than many writers seem to have realized. In an unpublished letter of 15 August 1953 Margerie Lowry wrote that it was in the 'next to final draft'. See UBC Box 3.

57 Robert Scholes, 'Metafiction', *The Iowa Review*, 1, 4 (Fall 1970), p. 107.

58 David Markson has asserted that 'Having known [Lowry] well in the last years of his life, I can venture that he would have contemplated mayhem before allowing the posthumous *Dark as the Grave Wherein My Friend is Laid* or *October Ferry to*

Gabriola to be published in that unrevised, patchwork form in which we have them', *Malcolm Lowry's 'Volcano'* (New York, 1978), p. viii. For an often persuasive critique of the Lowry editions see Matthew Corrigan, 'Malcolm Lowry, New York Publishing, and the "New Illiteracy"', *Encounter*, 35 (July 1970), pp. 82–93.

59 Lewis Carroll, *Alice's Adventures in Wonderland and Through the Looking-Glass* (Harmondsworth, 1974), p. 36.

60 Draft of 'Present Estate of Pompeii', UBC Box 24(17).

61 *Under the Volcano*, Central TV documentary, 15 May 1984.

62 For further discussion of these points see my forthcoming article on the film in *Critical Quarterly* (1984).

BIBLIOGRAPHY

WORKS BY MALCOLM LOWRY

Novels

Ultramarine. London: Jonathan Cape, 1933. Revised edition, Philadelphia, Pa: Lippincott, 1962. London: Jonathan Cape, 1963.

Under the Volcano. New York: Reynal & Hitchcock, 1947. London: Jonathan Cape, 1947.

Dark as the Grave Wherein My Friend is Laid. New York: New American Library, 1968. London: Jonathan Cape, 1969.

October Ferry to Gabriola. New York: World Publishing Company, 1970. London: Jonathan Cape, 1971.

Selected short fiction

'Port Swettenham'. *Experiment*, 3 (February 1930), pp. 22–6.

'Goya the Obscure'. *The Venture*, 6 (June 1930), pp. 270–8.

'Punctum Indifferens Skibet Gaar Videre'. *Experiment*, 7 (Spring 1931), pp. 62–75.

'In Le Havre'. *Life and Letters*, 10 (July 1934), pp. 462–6.

'Hotel Room in Chartres'. *Story*, 5 (September 1934), pp. 53–8.

'Economic Conference 1934'. *Arena*, 2 (Autumn 1949), pp. 49–57.

Hear Us O Lord from Heaven Thy Dwelling Place. Philadelphia, Pa: Lippincott, 1961. London: Jonathan Cape, 1962.

Lunar Caustic (ed. Earle Birney and Margerie Lowry). *Paris Review*, 29 (Winter/Spring 1963), pp. 15–72. London: Jonathan Cape, 1968.

'Bulls of the Resurrection'. *Prism International*, 5 (Summer 1965), pp. 5–11.

'Ghostkeeper'. *American Review*, 17 (May 1973), pp. 1–34.

Malcolm Lowry: Psalms and Songs (ed. Margerie Lowry). New York:

New American Library, 1975. (Includes 'China', 'June 30th, 1934!', 'Hotel Room in Chartres', 'Ghostkeeper' and *Lunar Caustic*.)

Poetry

Selected Poems of Malcolm Lowry (ed. Earle Birney). San Francisco, Ca: City Lights, 1962.

Selected non-fiction

Review of Earle Birney's *Turvey*. *Thunderbird*, 5 (December 1949), pp. 24–6.

'Garden of Etla'. *United Nations World*, 4 (June 1950), pp. 45–7.

'Preface to a Novel'. *Canadian Literature*, 9 (Summer 1961), pp. 23–9. Repr. in G. Woodcock (ed.), *Malcolm Lowry: The Man and his Work*, pp. 9–15.

The Selected Letters of Malcolm Lowry (ed. Harvey Breit and Margerie Lowry). Philadelphia, Pa: Lippincott, 1965. London: Jonathan Cape, 1967.

Notes on a Screenplay for F. Scott Fitzgerald's 'Tender is the Night' (with Margerie Bonner Lowry). Bloomfield Hills, Mich.: Bruccoli Clark, 1976.

Papers

The major Lowry manuscripts collection is held at the University of British Columbia; see J. O. Combs, *Malcolm Lowry: An Inventory of his Papers* . . . Vancouver: UBC, 1973.

BIBLIOGRAPHY

William H. New. *Malcolm Lowry: A Reference Guide*. Boston, Mass.: G. K. Hall, 1978.

J. Howard Woolmer. *Malcolm Lowry: A Bibliography*. Revere, Penn.: Woolmer/Brotherson, 1983.

See also the *Malcolm Lowry Newsletter*, published by the Department of English, Wilfrid Laurier University, Waterloo, Ontario.

SELECTED CRITICISM OF MALCOLM LOWRY

Books

Bradbrook, M. C. *Malcolm Lowry: His Art and Early Life*. London: Cambridge University Press, 1974.

Costa, Richard Hauer. *Malcolm Lowry*. New York: Twayne, 1972.

Cross, Richard K. *Malcolm Lowry: A Preface to his Fiction*. Chicago, Ill.: University of Chicago Press, 1980.

Day, Douglas. *Malcolm Lowry: A Biography*. New York: Oxford University Press, 1973. London: Oxford University Press, 1974.

Grace, Sherrill. *The Voyage That Never Ends: Malcolm Lowry's Fiction*. Vancouver: UBC Press, 1982.

New, William H. *Malcolm Lowry*. Toronto: McClelland & Stewart, 1971.

Smith, Anne (ed.). *The Art of Malcolm Lowry*. New York: Barnes & Noble, 1978. London: Vision Press, 1978.

Wood, Barry (ed.). *Malcolm Lowry: The Writer and his Critics*. Ottawa: Tecumseh Press, 1980.

Woodcock, George (ed.). *Malcolm Lowry: The Man and his Work*. Vancouver: UBC Press, 1971.

Guides to 'Under the Volcano'

Ackerley, Chris, and Clipper, Lawrence J. *A Guide to 'Under the Volcano'*. Vancouver: UBC Press, 1984.

Beckoff, Samuel. *Monarch Notes on 'Under the Volcano'*. New York: Monarch Press, 1975.

Markson, David. *Malcolm Lowry's 'Volcano': Myth, Symbol, Meaning*. New York: Times Books, 1978.

Articles

Baxter, Charles. 'The Escape from Irony: *Under the Volcano* and the Aesthetics of Arson'. *Novel*, 10 (Winter 1977), pp. 114–26.

Bradbury, Malcolm. 'Malcolm Lowry as Modernist'. In *Possibilities: Essays on the State of the Novel*, pp. 181–91. London: Oxford University Press, 1973.

Bromley, Roger. 'The Boundaries of Commitment: God, Lover, Comrade – Malcolm Lowry's *Under the Volcano* as a Reading of the 1930s'. In Francis Barker (ed.), *1936: The Sociology of Literature. Vol. I: The Politics of Modernism*, pp. 273–96. Colchester: University of Essex, 1979.

Corrigan, Matthew. 'Malcolm Lowry, New York Publishing, and the "New Illiteracy"'. *Encounter*, 35 (July 1970), pp. 82–93.

Cripps, Michael. '*Under the Volcano*: the Politics of the Imperial Self'. *Canadian Literature*, 95 (Winter 1982), pp. 85–101.

Edmonds, Dale. '*Under the Volcano*: a Reading of the "Immediate Level"'. *Tulane Studies in English*, 16 (1968), pp. 63–105.

Gass, William H. 'Malcolm Lowry'. In *The World Within the Word*, pp. 16–38. New York: Knopf, 1978.

Gilmore, Thomas B. 'The Place of Hallucinations in *Under the*

Volcano'. *Contemporary Literature*, 23, 3 (Summer 1982), pp. 285–305.

Perlmutter, Ruth. 'Malcolm Lowry's Unpublished Filmscript of *Tender is the Night*'. *American Quarterly*, 28 (1976), pp. 561–74.

Pottinger, Andrew J. 'The Consul's "Murder"'. *Canadian Literature*, 67 (Winter 1976), pp. 53–63.

Tiessen, Paul. 'Malcolm Lowry: Statements on Literature and Film'. In J. Campbell and J. Doyle (eds), *The Practical Vision: Essays in English Literature in Honour of Flora Roy*, pp. 119–32. Waterloo, Ontario: Wilfrid Laurier University Press, 1976.

Wain, John. 'Lowry's Subjective Equipment'. *The New Republic*, 154, 15 (January 1966), pp. 23–4.

—— 'Another Room in Hell'. *Atlantic Monthly* (August 1968), pp. 84–6.

Wainright, J. A. 'The Book "Being Written": Art and Life in *Dark as the Grave Wherein My Friend is Laid*'. *Dalhousie Review*, 59 (1979), pp. 82–104.

Walker, Ronald G. 'The *Barranca* of History' and 'Under *Under the Volcano*'. In *Infernal Paradise: Mexico and the Modern English Novel*, pp. 237–80 and 281–321. Los Angeles, Ca: University of California Press, 1978.

Wood, Barry. 'Malcolm Lowry's Metafiction: The Biography of a Genre'. *Contemporary Literature*, 19, 1 (Winter 1978), pp. 1–25. Reprinted in Wood (ed.), *Malcolm Lowry: The Writer and his Critics*, pp. 250–73.

York, Thomas. 'The Post-Mortem Point of View in Malcolm Lowry's *Under the Volcano*'. *Canadian Literature*, 99 (Winter 1983), pp. 35–46.